Home Organizing
& Closet Makeovers

A *Sunset* Design Guide

by Bridget Biscotti Bradley and the Editors of *Sunset*

Contents

Organizing your home and putting systems in place to keep it that way won't take as much time as you may think. Spend a couple of hours every weekend for a month, and you'll quickly see the benefits in the time you save not having to search for things you've misplaced. This book shows you how to tackle each room and every closet. Once you've removed the items you no longer need and assigned places for what is left, you'll find creative and attractive ways to display your belongings. Throughout the book, our design and organizing experts provide real-world advice and solutions. These professionals have helped thousands of clients get organized with style. Now they're sharing their secrets with us.

20

60

A Well-Organized Home
page 6

 8 | Kitchens
10 | Bathrooms
12 | Family and Dining Rooms
14 | Bedrooms
16 | Closets
18 | Work Spaces

Kitchens
page 20

22 | Existing Kitchens
24 | Quick and Easy Solutions
36 | Kitchen Islands
38 | Designing a New Kitchen

Bathrooms
page 44

46 | Vanities
50 | Freestanding Furniture
52 | Toiletries and Towels
56 | Laundry and Trash
58 | Tub and Shower Areas

Family and Dining Rooms
page 60

62 | Gathering Areas
70 | Displaying Collections
74 | Bookshelves
78 | Dining Rooms
82 | Displaying Photos

Bedrooms
page 86

88 | Personal Retreats
96 | Guest Rooms
98 | Nurseries
102 | Kids' Rooms

Closets
page 108

110 | Reorganizing Your Closet
112 | Closet Systems
114 | Hall and Utility Closets
116 | Bedroom Closets
124 | Kids' Closets
126 | Teens' Closets

Work Spaces
page 128

130 | Home Offices
138 | Alternative Work Areas
142 | Small-Space Work Areas

Entries and Mudrooms
page 146

148 | Entryways
154 | Back Doors
156 | Mudrooms

Laundry and Craft Rooms
page 158

160 | Laundry Rooms
166 | Craft Spaces

Getting It Done
page 170

172 | Purging and Organizing
176 | Getting Help
178 | Budget Solutions
182 | Specialized Storage

Resources | 186
Photography Credits | 188
Index | 190

©2010 by Time Home Entertainment Inc.
135 West 50th Street, New York, NY 10020

ISBN-13: 978-0-376-00590-8
ISBN-10: 0-376-00590-4
Library of Congress Control Number: 2009937368

10 9 8 7 6 5 4 3 2 1
First Printing July 2010
Printed in the United States of America

OXMOOR HOUSE
VP, *Publishing Director:* Jim Childs
Editorial Director: Susan Payne Dobbs
Brand Manager: Fonda Hitchcock
Managing Editor: Laurie S. Herr

SUNSET PUBLISHING
President: Barb Newton
VP, Editor-in-Chief: Katie Tamony
Creative Director: Mia Daminato

*Home Organizing & Closet Makeovers:
A Sunset Design Guide*
CONTRIBUTORS
Author: Bridget Biscotti Bradley
Managing Editor: Bob Doyle
Photo Editor: Philippine Scali
Production Specialist: Linda M. Bouchard
Proofreader: John Edmonds
Indexer: Marjorie Joy
Series Designer: Vasken Guiragossian

To order additional publications, call 1-800-765-6400

For more books to enrich your life, visit oxmoorhouse.com

Visit Sunset online at sunset.com

For the most comprehensive selection of Sunset books, visit sunsetbooks.com

For more exciting home and garden ideas, visit myhomeideas.com

Cover Photo: Photography by Ericka McConnell; styling by Philippine Scali; Trivino Binder and Havana Archival Box by Kolo (Kolo.com)

Design Panel

The following professionals from across the United States contributed ideas and expertise.

Celia Tejada
SENIOR VICE PRESIDENT, PRODUCT DESIGN AND DEVELOPMENT, POTTERY BARN KIDS & PBTEEN

Celia Tejada has spent 29 years in the design industry, including nine years as the head of her own clothing company, six years as an interior designer, and the past 14 years with the Pottery Barn division of Williams-Sonoma, Inc. During her tenure, she has been the driving force behind the simple designs and casual comfort that epitomize the Pottery Barn style. Tejada has been featured in publications that run the global gamut from *Women's Wear Daily* to *House Beautiful, Spazio Casa, Designing Women, Food & Wine, House & Garden, Elle Decor,* and *Fast Company.* She has also been featured on television, including design and lifestyle programs on A&E, *Oprah, Designing with Confidence,* and *House Beautiful* on E! Tejada was born and raised in northern Spain and graduated from the International School of Design in Bilbao.

Kit Davey
INTERIOR DESIGNER

Kit Davey's mission is to create beauty, harmony, and order in her clients' homes. She has transformed thousands of households since she started her business in 1991. Her company, A Fresh Look, provides room makeovers, design advice, staging, and professional organizing services. Davey is an allied member of A.S.I.D., a licensed realtor, a feng shui practitioner, and a member of the National Association of Professional Organizers. She is also a syndicated design columnist and teaches design, organizing, and staging in the San Francisco area.
www.AFreshLook.net

Monica Ricci
PROFESSIONAL ORGANIZER

Monica Ricci is a Certified Professional Organizer©, the author of *Organize Your Office in No Time,* and an avid blogger based in Atlanta, Georgia. She appears frequently as an industry expert on radio and television. Ricci consults with companies such as Beazer Homes, Rubbermaid, 3M, Office Depot, and Dymo, and she can be seen on the HGTV show *MISSION: Organization.* She loves public speaking and inspiring other people to create simple, joyful, powerful lives. | **www.catalystorganizing.com**

Deborah Silberberg and Sylvia Borchert
PROFESSIONAL ORGANIZERS

Deborah Silberberg has been working with individual clients for 25 years—first on bookkeeping and financial management and later through her professional organizing company, ShipShape. Sylvia Borchert joined the company in 1994, bringing an extensive background in event planning. Together they have expanded ShipShape into a full-service organizing consulting company, with offices in Oakland and New York. They work with a team of professionals from varied backgrounds in areas such as art, catering, computers, design, and office management. ShipShape has been featured on HGTV and NPR, as well as in numerous publications, including *The San Francisco Chronicle*. | **www.shipshape.com**

Lori Dennis
INTERIOR DESIGNER

Lori Dennis graduated from UCLA's interior design program and formed the Los Angeles–based Dennis Design Group in 1998, specializing in green interior design. Her eco-friendly projects include residential, commercial, and hospitality interiors throughout the nation. Dennis' work has been featured in numerous print and online publications, including *The New York Times, Coastal Living, Southern Accents, Woman's Day, Los Angeles Times, California Homes, Angeleno*, and *Dwell*. She has been recognized for outstanding green and modern design by A.S.I.D., *Home* magazine, *Southern Accents, California Homes*, and *Angeleno* magazine. Dennis has also been a featured expert on HGTV, Food Network, Oxygen Network, NBC, KABC, and XM Radio. **www.dennisdesigngroup.com**

Jen M. R. Doman
PROFESSIONAL ORGANIZER

Jen Doman has been transforming spaces and producing events since 2004. She is the founder and president of Manhattan-based Get It Together, which provides organizational services for homes, offices, estates, and events. Get It Together has been singled out in print and media outlets such as *New York* magazine, *O at Home, Redbook*, HGTV, Oprah.com, *Apartment Therapy*, and *Martha Stewart Radio*, among others. Doman is a native New Yorker who graduated from Hobart and William Smith Colleges. She earned a master's degree from the Medill School of Journalism at Northwestern University. | **www.getit-together.com**

Sara Eizen
PROFESSIONAL ORGANIZER

Sara Eizen is the owner of Nest, a Seattle-based interior design, home organizing, and color consultation company that helps busy moms and new parents add style and space to their homes on any budget. As the mother of young twins, Eizen knows the toll that kid chaos can take on a grown-up's sense of style and order. That's why she offers creative, affordable ways to make homes look, feel, and function the way their owners want, no matter how many kids are running underfoot. Eizen has a degree in interior design from Michigan State University. **www.nestseattle.com**

Kate Parker
DESIGN CONSULTANT

Kate Parker specializes in creating spaces with both style and functionality. She is a contributor to *Real Simple*, where she spent three years on staff as an editor before branching out on her own. She can now be found blogging on RealSimple.com, styling stories for the magazine, and executing home makeovers. Parker has appeared as a design expert on *Today* and *The Early Show*. She lives in West Palm Beach, Florida. **www.ParkersAtHome.com**

Chapter 1

A Well-Organized Home

After a long day at a hectic pace, everyone should be able to find relief in a clean, well-organized home. When there's a place for everything and everything is in its place, you will be able to stay calm and relaxed. No more searching through piles of paperwork for a missing bill or running from room to room looking for the keys when you're already late for work. Throughout this book you will find specific ideas to organize each room of the house. The spaces shown in this first chapter present a mix of resourcefulness, practicality, and creative design to aim for.

Turn a dining room
wall into functional
storage space that's
visually appealing.

Frosted glass cabinet doors give a glimpse of color while disguising package labeling that doesn't need to be on display. The island in this kitchen provides a large chopping-block surface, complete with a cutout for disposing of waste.

"Right now people aren't travelling or eating out as much as they once did. They realize that as long as they're going to be at home all the time, they owe it to themselves to get organized."

—Jen M. R. Doman, professional organizer

ABOVE A mix of open shelves in vertical and horizontal configurations provides the setting for an artful display of wine bottles and accessories.

RIGHT See-through containers keep staples fresh and easy to find in this highly practical pantry.

FAR RIGHT Instead of hiding them behind closed doors, display collections of cake stands or teacups on open shelves in kitchens or dining rooms.

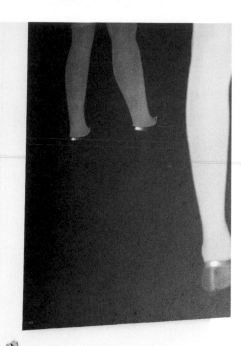

"The key to organizing is to edit, then sort, then place. If you don't have room for it, don't love it, or don't use it, donate it." —Kit Davey, interior designer

A vintage chair next to a pink claw-foot tub gives you a place to sit while you're helping a child at bath time, and it can also hold towels and a book during your bath.

Hooks on the wall
and baskets under
the sink keep a
plentiful supply of
towels within reach.

Bookshelves surrounding the entry from a living room to a dining room make creative use of what might otherwise be under-utilized wall space.

ABOVE Small-home living requires creative—sometimes even eccentric—storage solutions. Bicycles held up by a system of pulleys hover above this comfortable living room.

LEFT A floating wall shelf positioned above a cabinet gives you an extra level for displaying art and collectibles.

"Start by coming up with a goal for the space. Write it down or find a picture that captures it. If along the way the process becomes difficult, remind yourself of that goal."
—Kate Parker, design consultant

Open shelves outfitted with baskets encourage children to put their toys away. Assign lower shelves to the young ones and upper shelves to their elder siblings.

A wall of built-in cabinets over the bed maximizes storage space and keeps the room serene.

Hooks for items in daily use, strategically placed on the door of the entry closet, will save you from having to search for them each time you leave the house.

"Put like items together and assign a place for everything. Designating a home for each item is the key to not having to search down the line."
—Sylvia Borchert, professional organizer

ABOVE Widely available storage systems can help you organize a built-in closet or fashion a closet where none existed before.

RIGHT Storing shoes on shelves in plain view makes it easier to grab the right pair and go.

FAR RIGHT The cavernous closets prized by adults are of little practical use for children's clothing. Use them for your own things while the kids are young, and put the kids' tiny outfits into a freestanding armoire.

"There is no quick fix. Attack one area at a time, a couple of hours at a time. Eventually you'll get to everything."
—Sara Eizen, professional organizer

Personalize your work area with a large cutout made of wood or cork. It can double as a place to post notes.

Art and collectibles warm up a home office, but you need to keep them from obstructing your work. Floating wall shelves above the desk are an ideal solution.

Chapter 2

Kitchens

Basic organizing principles, such as regularly thinning out your possessions, grouping similar items, and keeping the things you use most frequently visible and within reach, are crucial in a kitchen because it is the hub of so much activity. Meal preparation and cleanup happen there two or three times a day, kids do their homework and grab quick snacks, and parents look for recipes on their laptops or pay bills on a corner of the tabletop. It's a space in constant motion. The ideas in this chapter will help you make your kitchen run like a well-oiled machine.

A combination of open and closed storage in this kitchen allows for maximum flexibility.

Existing Kitchens

Working in a kitchen where everything is in its place makes meal preparation faster.

Do you feel like the work you do in your kitchen isn't as efficient as it should be? Are you constantly searching for the tools you need or juggling spice jars with messy hands in the middle of a recipe? Have some of your kitchen drawers become depositories for odds and ends that simply don't seem to have a home anywhere else? The following pages will provide solutions to basic storage and organization problems that can be accomplished without the expense of remodeling the room. If you are planning a remodcl to update the room or solve floor plan issues, see pages 36 through 43 for ideas on new kitchen design.

Purge First, Ask Questions Later

The first step to a kitchen that runs like clockwork is to have essential items close at hand and rarely used items tucked away. Start by spending a Saturday taking everything out of the drawers and cabinets. Wipe down all surfaces, while the drawers and shelves are empty, using a mild, nontoxic cleaner, such as a solution of water and white vinegar. Take this opportunity to discard or compost any food items that have gone bad, make a box of canned goods you can't see yourself using in the next few months for donation to a local food bank, and think about a similar charitable contribution of any cookware or small appliances that you never use. Also separate out any seldom used but essential seasonal items, such as holiday cookie cutters, decorative platters, and teacups too delicate for regular rotation.

Group like items together, then put them away as close as possible to where they will be used. For example, store glasses near the refrigerator or your source for filtered water. Keep plates and silverware near the dishwasher so you're not crossing the kitchen to unload the machine. Put cookie sheets and casseroles near the oven, pots and pans near the stovetop. Read on for more specific solutions.

TOP RIGHT Put a message board for important phone numbers or to-do lists in the kitchen where the entire family will see it throughout the day.

BOTTOM RIGHT If you have the right space, turn an existing lower cabinet into a feeding station for the pets so you can avoid tripping over their bowls. Remove the cabinet doors and put bowls for food and water on the lowest shelf and a basket for leashes and toys above. Extra food can be stored in a lidded container.

Quick and Easy Solutions

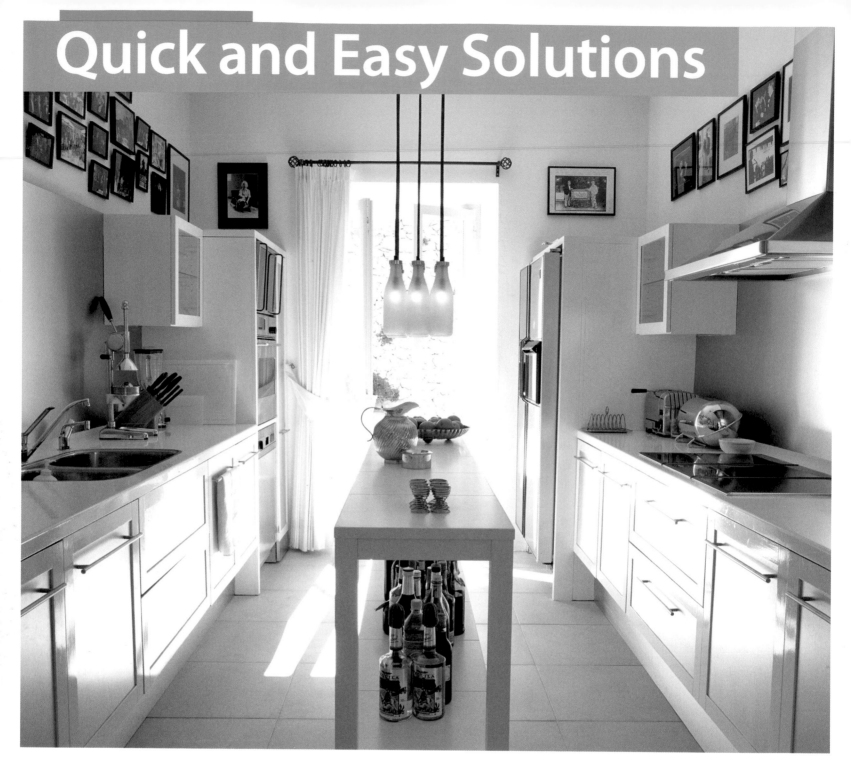

Go to any storage or kitchen supply store and you'll find dozens of accessories for organizing food and cookware in pantries or drawers, on shelves or counters, or hanging from the ceiling. "My clients usually want to go out and buy these storage solutions before doing the first step of purging and organizing," cautions professional organizer Jen M. R. Doman. "In many cases, people have the majority of what they need, but it's just not being well utilized. So I encourage them not to go shopping until we have a clear plan for the kitchen, so they only buy what they need." Make a list of all the items you've gathered during your kitchen purge that need a better organizing solution. That way you'll know what the problems are as you peruse the aisles.

On the Counter

Organize the countertop and create more space for cooking by gathering fruit in a single bowl and storing bread in a box that will extend its shelf life. Place the items you use every day on a turntable or tray that groups them visually and protects the countertop. Cooking utensils such as spatulas and whisks can be stashed in drawers, but it may be more efficient to keep the tools you use most often beside the stove in a utensil holder.

In Drawers

With little expense, you can make quick work of messy drawers. Use dividers to separate items so you can see all the contents at a glance. Mix and match modular drawer dividers based on the size of the things you're storing. Corral smaller items, such as napkin rings and rubber bands, in see-through containers or baskets so they don't migrate to the back of the drawer. Any shallow box or letter-sized envelope can organize your take-out menus or kitchen appliance manuals; they'll be even easier to find alphabetized in a binder.

In Cabinets

Lower cabinets are often the trouble spots in kitchens. You can't see to the back of the cabinet without getting down on the floor, so you tend to pile things in front and forget about what's in back. A better solution is to outfit the cabinets with pullout organizers. Make sure you buy sliding shelves that are rated to handle the weight of the items you plan to store. Professional organizer Monica Ricci notes: "If retrofitting with pullout shelves and baskets is beyond your budget, apply battery-operated press-on lights in base cabinets so you can at least see what's back there."

Lazy Susans can make items reachable at the back of upper and lower cabinets. Stacking shelves allow you to store more cups or dishes in upper cabinets and to see small items that might otherwise be forgotten behind larger ones. There are also bins that attach underneath a shelf that maximize space between fixed shelves without stacking things too high. And don't forget the insides of cabinet doors: Install racks or narrow baskets to hold packages of snacks or instant oatmeal, or the lids of containers.

OPPOSITE PAGE Knife holders, bread bins, and fruit trays keep countertops organized, while well-planned cabinets facilitate clutter control.

TOP Instead of keeping boxes of snacks on the counter, transfer the contents into lidded glass containers. This will make the countertop look less cluttered and also keep the snacks fresh longer.

BOTTOM LEFT Make junk drawers a thing of the past by using dividers and small containers to keep things organized and instantly accessible.

BOTTOM RIGHT Store-bought wire pullout shelves turn awkwardly dark lower cabinets into useful and accessible storage space. Side-mount baskets like the ones shown are good for light loads, while bottom-mount rails are better for heavy things.

PROFESSIONAL ORGANIZER
JEN M. R. DOMAN ON

In and Out Boxes

The kitchen is the hub of the home, so mail and keys inevitably get dumped there when people come in. Every household should have two boxes in the kitchen that are no more than 5 by 11 inches. Put incoming mail in one and anything that needs to leave with you in the other. At the end of each week, take the boxes to the couch and put everything where it needs to go, so you have empty boxes again on Monday.

Hanging Racks

Use the surface beneath upper cabinets to hang stemware on racks, or mugs on hooks. Hanging-rail systems can be installed behind the sink or stove to keep utensils, spices, and paper towels off the countertop. Hooks can be added or removed from the rails as needed. If you have limited cabinet space, pots and pans can hang from a rack on the ceiling. Pot racks keep things easy to see and reach while you're preparing a meal.

Around the Sink

When the area around the kitchen sink is cluttered, washing the dishes becomes more of a chore. Keep the surrounding countertop clear by using a caddy for dish soap, hand soap, and hand lotion. Paper towels can be on a freestanding holder, tucked under an upper cabinet, or on a roll attached to the door of the cabinet directly under the sink. Having the paper towels mounted on something makes it easier to tear off a sheet with wet hands. Professional organizer Sara Eizen notes that many of her clients buy cleaning supplies in bulk. Instead of large plastic containers next to the sink, she recommends

pretty olive oil dispensers for liquid soap and detergent. "Refill the dispensers as needed and put the large containers in the garage so they don't take up valuable space under the kitchen sink," Eizen says.

Your cloth dish towels need a proper place to dry. A pullout rack or bar installed under the sink keeps them close at hand. This simple and inexpensive solution keeps wet towels from being messily draped over the faucet or oven handle. Keep fresh ones stacked in a nearby drawer and swap them out every few days.

Sponges left on the counter don't dry properly, encouraging bacteria to grow. Avoid the problem by placing wet sponges in an open basket that attaches to the inside of the sink. Or place the sponges on a layer of cork stoppers that absorb the excess liquid. Sponges should not be kept in use for more than a few weeks. A more environmentally friendly solution to avoid discarding so many sponges is to use small white towels to wash the dishes, then launder the towels once or twice a week. There are also reusable, quick-dry microfiber pads that can be cleaned in the dishwasher.

OPPOSITE PAGE, LEFT Pans hang within arm's reach above the cooktop.

OPPOSITE PAGE, RIGHT A coat rack holds pots and pans in this kitchen. Lids fit perfectly between hooks.

ABOVE LEFT A wooden rack mounted above the sink allows dishes to drip-dry without taking up counter space.

ABOVE RIGHT Use baskets and bins to keep the area under the sink from getting out of control.

Under the Sink

Keep cleaning supplies organized with pullout racks or Lazy Susans. Large bulk containers should stay towards the back, while the items you most often need to take with you about the house can be kept in a small tote. There are pullout racks made specifically to fit around plumbing supply pipes and garbage disposals. If you have small children in the house, be sure to install childproof locks on under-sink cabinet doors or find another location for storing the cleaning supplies.

PROFESSIONAL ORGANIZER
SARA EIZEN ON

Space Under the Sink

I recommend keeping only things you will access on a weekly basis under the sink. It's preferable to put garbage cans somewhere else, but if you must have one under the sink, install a bottom-mounted, pullout wire rack in the cabinet and put your trash can on one side and baskets or buckets to contain dishwashing and kitchen cleaning supplies on the other. If you buy garbage bags in bulk, keep a few extra bags in the trash can lying flat under the bag you're currently using so you always have one at hand and put the box in the garage.

Dishes and Glassware

Open shelves invite more artistic stacks of plates, organized by color and size, while dishes stored behind closed doors are all about efficiency. Get the most out of the space between shelves with boosters that ensure you don't stack anything too high to be easily accessible. Plate racks hold plates on their sides so they don't touch. They may be overkill for everyday plates, but they help protect the finish of fine china or antique dishes. Professional organizer Deborah Silberberg suggests having only six place settings in rotation stored close at hand. "Put the other four or six sets up higher or toward the back of a cabinet if you only use them when company comes over. That way," she advises, "the stacks of dishes won't get so awkwardly high and heavy."

Store glasses by size, stacking when you can. Delicate wine and martini glasses can stand on their own or hang from racks under shelves or cabinets. Don't overcrowd the area, or you may chip delicate glassware. Mugs and teacups are excellent candidates for hanging by their handles.

Silverware, Knives, and Cooking Utensils

Drawer dividers make organizing silverware a breeze and are available in various configurations, including expandable, deep-drawer, and stacking varieties. Most have separate dividers for small and large forks, small and large spoons, and butter knives. If you have an extra drawer, get another divider for steak knives, grapefruit spoons, iced-tea spoons, and other specialty silverware. Or if you have deep enough drawers, you can stack two drawer dividers to keep the pieces you use most often on top.

Knife collections often come with their own wood blocks that are meant to be kept on the kitchen countertop. They keep blades sharp and are safer than having the knives float around loose in a drawer. Other options are to store knives in separate sliding trays on top of other utensils or in a shallow pullout shelf of their own. To keep them away from young children, consider a drop-down rack mounted under an upper cabinet, or a magnetic rack on the wall adjacent to the food-preparation area.

Cooking utensils can also be organized with drawer dividers. Group like-sized items together, since you may have only one or two of each tool. Baking utensils such as wooden spoons and whisks can be stored together, while long barbecue forks and skewers can go in a separate container. Dry-ingredient measuring cups should stack one inside the next. Keep them together by threading a string through openings in the handles.

ABOVE Open shelves display a mix-match set of dishes with varying patterns but complementary colors. Small teacups hang on hooks under the bottom shelf.

OPPOSITE PAGE, TOP LEFT Drawer dividers can help with many kitchen tools. Rolling pins, spatulas, and measuring cups can fit in wide dividers, making it much easier to find what you're looking for.

OPPOSITE PAGE, TOP RIGHT Display and functionality combine in this arrangement of white ceramic dishes.

OPPOSITE PAGE, BOTTOM LEFT Magnetic knife racks keep these sharp instruments within safe reach. Above, plate dividers display flatware and prevent chipped edges by keeping individual pieces separated.

OPPOSITE PAGE, BOTTOM RIGHT Deep and wide drawer dividers hold dozens of utensils and make things easier to find.

Pots, Pans, and Trays

It can be a challenge to keep pots and pans tidy, but if you spend some time coming up with an organization plan that works for what you actually own and use, you'll find the area won't get disorderly as quickly. Deep drawers are the best places to store these large, bulky items. You can use drawer separators to keep lids from migrating over to the pots, and you'll never have to reach to the back of the shelf to find what you are looking for. If you don't have over-sized drawers, invest in a pullout shelf organizer with racks for large baking sheets and lids, flat areas for pots, and wide separators for pans. If you store trays, cookie sheets, and pans vertically, you avoid having to pull out the bottom one at risk of toppling all the others.

Spices and Staples

There are dozens of organizing methods for spices; the plan you choose should be based on the number of spices you tend to have at one time and how often you use them. Spices kept in a cool, dry place away from direct sunlight will last the longest. If stored correctly, dried herbs can last one to three years, ground spices two to three years, seasoning blends one to two years, and extracts about four years. Whole spices last longer than pre-ground varieties—roughly three to four years—and the intensity of flavor is greater when you grind spices to order. Mark the date on the bottom of spice jars so you know how long you've had them. Stale spices won't make you sick; they just lose their flavor over time.

If you tend to use the same spices almost every time you cook, it can be useful to keep those next to or above the stove. They won't last as long, being near a heat source, but it probably won't matter if you go through them quickly. Cooks who tend to have large numbers of spices benefit from angled drawer inserts. For spices stored in a cabinet, tiered shelves allow you to see the back row. Alternatively, you can mount a spice rack to the inside of the cabinet door, as the bottles are light and narrow. Spinning spice racks keep a limited number of containers organized on the counter-top. Whichever system you choose, try to keep the jars alphabetized or arranged by cuisine so you can quickly find exactly what you need.

OPPOSITE PAGE, TOP LEFT Vertical dividers keep cake pans and casserole trays easy to see and retrieve. Use any leftover slots for your go-to cookbooks or food magazines.

OPPOSITE PAGE, BOTTOM LEFT Wide, deep drawers are ideal for storing pots and pans, as they can accommodate long handles.

OPPOSITE PAGE, RIGHT Reminiscent of test tubes in a lab, these cork-topped glass vials make finding the right spice quick and easy. Date each spice so you know when to replace it.

RIGHT Narrow shelves above the cooktop keep the spices and oils you use every night within easy reach. Store things you don't use regularly away from the heat.

LEFT A high ceiling allows this creative wine storage idea. Small cutouts high up on the wall keep bottles horizontal, dark, and cool. A narrow ladder hangs on the wall when not in use and can easily be moved to the metal rod running under the storage area.

OPPOSITE PAGE, TOP If you have space above your upper cabinets, decorative wooden boxes used to ship nice wines will give the kitchen a rustic wine cellar look.

OPPOSITE PAGE, BOTTOM LEFT There are a variety of small racks and shelves on the market that will allow you to keep your short-term wine supply correctly oriented and organized in the kitchen. The Holman Entertaining Shelves from Pottery Barn hold six bottles and include wooden glides for hanging accompanying wineglasses.

OPPOSITE PAGE, BOTTOM RIGHT This pullout wire shelf moves in two parts. When you open the door, the shelves immediately inside come out into the room, and two shelves that take up the back corner of the cabinet are pulled forward so you can view the contents. For items you use every day, it's the best way to access the back corner.

Wine

Storing wine is about more than just where to put all those bottles. Wine must be kept horizontal so the corks do not dry out, and it does best in stable temperatures away from sunlight. The storage area should not vibrate from nearby appliances or slamming doors, and the bottles shouldn't be stored near items with strong odors. The ideal temperature for wine that is to be kept for more than six months is 50 to 55 degrees Fahrenheit; humidity should be 70 percent or higher to keep corks moist and minimize evaporation. Basement wine cellars with light, temperature, and humidity controls are a wine lover's dream, but collectors who don't have such a space do fine with specialized wine refrigerators that maintain proper humidity and keep the temperature in the right range.

Bottles that you plan to consume within three to six months can be kept in an interior closet where they will be cool, dark, and undisturbed. There are also a number of wine storage solutions specific to kitchens. The best place for longer-term storage is under upper cabinets that are away from windows, the stove, the dishwasher, or any other heat-producing or vibrating appliance. Unless your kitchen is quite large, however, it may be easier to find a lower cabinet for the bottles.

Making the Best Use of Corners

Lower cabinets that come to a corner are a storage challenge. Thirty years ago, the best you could do to ensure that nothing got lost was to install a lazy Susan. Today, however, there are a variety of pullout or pivot-and-turn hardware solutions that can be added to existing cabinetry. Before deciding which to buy, consider what you're planning to store in the cabinet, then find hardware that meets the weight and size requirements. One low cost solution is to stow seldom-used seasonal items in that difficult-to-reach back corner, tucked in a zippered bag or basket with a handle that can be used to retrieve the items. But for things that you need to use more often, outfitting the cabinet with a system that allows you to avoid getting on your hands and knees can be a worthwhile investment.

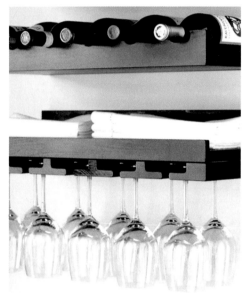

PROFESSIONAL ORGANIZER
SYLVIA BORCHERT ON

Wine Tags

I suggest keeping a small bag for wine hang tags and a pen where your wine is stored, so that you can immediately label the wine bottles as you put them in their horizontal racks. That way you can see quickly the contents of a bottle without pulling it out. If you have a row of the same kind of wine, just put the tag on the first bottle in the row.

Organizing the Pantry

Walk-in pantries are a rarity in small homes. If you're lucky enough to have one, you'll want to keep it well organized to maximize usable space. Buying food in bulk can save money, especially if you're able to keep it fresh for months at a time. Transfer dry food into glass jars with airtight tops so you can see how much there is left. Better yet, take reusable bags to the grocery store and buy from bulk bins, then transfer to glass or metal containers when you get home. In this way, you won't have any packaging to throw out.

The same principles apply when you use a floor-to-ceiling cabinet or free-standing bookshelf as a pantry. When shelves are deep, consider outfitting a few of them with pullout wire shelves. Baskets keep things looking organized in a pantry that isn't hidden behind doors. Narrow floor-to-ceiling cabinets are great for storing canned goods and staples in small jars. You can attach sliding shelves to the inside of the cabinet door so that the shelves come out into the room when the door is pulled open. Or install narrow metal racks on the inside of cabinet doors.

Trash and Recycling Areas

Kitchen garbage should be kept in a lidded container or in a slide-out cabinet placed as close to the food-preparation area as possible. While one trash can per kitchen used to be the norm, now many kitchens have two or more receptacles for glass and plastic recycling, paper recycling, composting, and remainders destined for the landfill. You are more likely to recycle properly if you can sort the materials at the source. If you can't make room for everything, try to add at least one container for the material you recycle the most.

OPPOSITE PAGE, LEFT This closet off the kitchen was converted for use as a food pantry. Deep shelves hold cans, boxes, and glass containers, and the countertop on a lower cabinet holds the microwave, so it doesn't take up valuable space in the kitchen.

OPPOSITE PAGE, RIGHT A pantry on an exterior wall is kept cool naturally with screened louvers that let in the outside air. It's the perfect way to store staples like grains and nuts, and even the butter you use every day.

ABOVE LEFT A rolling, lidded trash can fits nicely in an empty space between two base cabinets. It can easily be moved to the kitchen table for peeling potatoes or next to the sink for scraping dishes.

ABOVE RIGHT In addition to your main kitchen trash can, try to find room for pullout cans to hold glass, metal, and paper recycling.

INTERIOR DESIGNER
LORI DENNIS ON

Composing

These days, more and more people are deciding to compost food waste rather than add to overcrowded landfills. There are lots of attractive lidded containers you can store on your countertop. If you have two sinks or two food-prep areas, put a compost bin at each station. Some European cabinetmakers have integrated compost areas into stock cabinet designs. But to get something like that here, you'll likely need to go to a custom cabinetmaker. The key is to design a solution that's seamless enough to use regularly without thinking about it.

Kitchen Islands

The curved shape of this island welcomes guests into the kitchen to take part in the action.

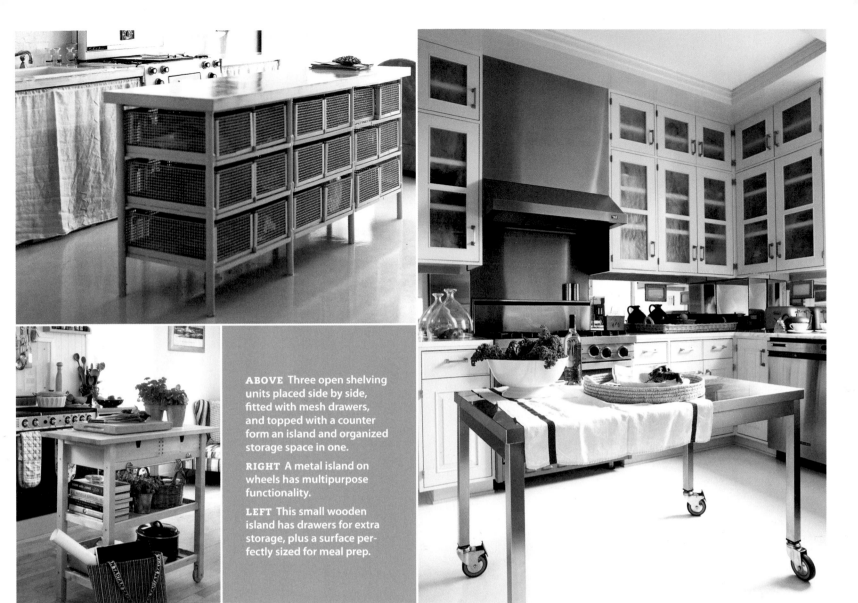

ABOVE Three open shelving units placed side by side, fitted with mesh drawers, and topped with a counter form an island and organized storage space in one.

RIGHT A metal island on wheels has multipurpose functionality.

LEFT This small wooden island has drawers for extra storage, plus a surface perfectly sized for meal prep.

Adding an island increases storage and countertop space in the kitchen. It's much less expensive to add such a unit than to remodel the entire room. If you have the floor space, you can add a small fixed island in the center of a U-shaped kitchen. Or when all you need is a little more counter space during preparation of large meals, you might choose a small island on wheels that can be parked adjacent to your base cabinets and moved away when not needed. For a big change that's still a notch below a full remodel, consider replacing one wall of your kitchen with an island. This will open the kitchen up to the living or dining room; it can even include a breakfast bar that serves as a place to gather or eat a quick meal.

Think through your storage needs before settling on the size and design of a kitchen island. If you want one with an integral sink, there may need to be a trash area as part of the island. Narrow islands with open shelves underneath are useful for storing small appliances like stand mixers and blenders. Incorporate a microwave or space for your cookbook collection on the end of a larger island.

PROFESSIONAL ORGANIZER
JEN M. R. DOMAN ON

Cleaning Out the Fridge

Schedule 20 minutes at the end of one day each week to deal with what's in the refrigerator. If you don't take the time to decide whether you'll ever eat that take-out food, it will likely stay there for months, using up space in the back. You'll save money too, both by not buying things you already have but couldn't see and by not paying to cool things you don't really need to save.

Designing a New Kitchen

Drawers below and a mix of solid and glass cabinet doors above give you the best range of options. Food is kept behind closed doors, while plates and glasses can be put on display.

When you're about to embark on a kitchen remodel that involves new cabinetry, you owe it to yourself to make sure you wind up with a well-organized work space. It's crucial to plan for storage needs before you place the cabinet order. Go through the purging process described on page 23 to see what you have and what you might get rid of. Group like items together and figure out where you most often use each category of kitchen paraphernalia, so you can store things as close to that spot as possible.

As you're leafing through catalogs that show the hundreds of products designed to organize the contents of your kitchen, remember that more isn't always better. You can end up spending thousands of dollars on systems that might not make as big a difference as a few well-chosen pieces and a thoughtful kitchen design.

Professional organizer Deborah Silberberg always asks clients who in the household does most of the cooking and whether that person is left or right handed. Drawers should be installed where it makes the most sense for the person who is cooking day in and day out. "If two people cook and one is left handed while the other is right handed, put in a drawer separator so that each person can comfortably grab utensils," Silberberg says.

Efficient Work Spaces

If you aren't working with a kitchen designer, review the National Kitchen and Bath Association's guidelines for creating an efficient work space at www. nkba.org. You will find information on proper heights and clearances, work triangles, solutions for various kitchen floor plans, and how much counter space you should have next to sinks and appliances.

TOP Design all of the base cabinets with pullouts, whether drawers or shelves. Deep drawers can be used for everything from pots and pans to plates and bowls.

BOTTOM LEFT Design space for a chair in a run of base cabinets or in an island, and use the area for bill paying or homework. A microwave on an open shelf to the side of the chair gives kids easy access to heat up their own snacks after school.

BOTTOM RIGHT New custom cabinets allow you to utilize every inch of space, including the toe-kick area.

INTERIOR DESIGNER
KIT DAVEY ON

Solutions for Kids and Pets

When you're designing a kitchen from scratch, you can think outside the box. Dog and cat owners can create feeding areas in one of the base cabinets and even install a small faucet to avoid walking the water bowl across the kitchen. Put a shelf on one side for food and a hook for the scoop. For kids, create a snack station with the foods they're allowed to eat ready at hand, so they won't need help from an adult. Add a low microwave, if you choose.

Open Storage and Display

One of the many decisions you'll make in designing a new kitchen is whether you want open or closed cabinets. Both have their advantages, and it really comes down to the style you prefer and the way you use your kitchen.

In a small space, installing open shelves rather than upper cabinets makes the room feel larger. Contents of open shelves will gather dust over time, however. If you store dishes and glassware that you use and clean frequently, this isn't a major concern. But decorative dishes or rarely used bakeware stored on open shelves will need regular dusting and cleaning before use. If you have a beautiful collection of pottery or your grandmother's dishes, on the other hand, open-shelf display is a great solution—it will make your collections feel more accessible.

Pantry items such as canned goods and boxed cereals can also be stored on open shelves, but this is a more informal look. If seeing different sizes and colors on the shelf bothers you, consider cabinets with cloudy or wavy glass doors. They will provide a lighter, brighter look than solid wood doors but obscure the shapes and the advertising copy on cans and boxes. An alternative is to transfer the contents to glass jars and arrange like colors together on the open shelves to create artistic displays.

INTERIOR DESIGNER
LORI DENNIS ON

Choosing Open Shelves

A big part of eco-friendly design is using what you have, so when a client wants a new look but their current cabinets are functional, we suggest taking the doors off some cabinets. This adds virtual square footage in small kitchens because the visual depth is increased, and it makes things easier to reach and utilize. When I see things frequently, like platters or a glass container of granola, I'm more likely to use or eat what I can see. Exposed things prompt action, but when things are tucked away, you tend to forget about them.

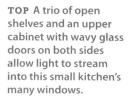

TOP A trio of open shelves and an upper cabinet with wavy glass doors on both sides allow light to stream into this small kitchen's many windows.

BOTTOM LEFT Use shelves at eye level to display your favorite dishes. Stack them in varying heights.

BOTTOM RIGHT An open bookshelf is a great way to add storage space in a kitchen.

OPPOSITE PAGE Shelves are made more useful with baskets that pull all the way out.

RIGHT A collection of white ceramics is kept clean but is still on view from both the kitchen and the dining room through clear glass doors.

BELOW LEFT Frosted glass doors obscure shelf contents and break up an expanse of solid cabinetry.

BELOW RIGHT Small baking supplies are easily accessible in pullout drawers.

Closed Storage Solutions

People who cook infrequently or who want to minimize the dusting necessitated by open shelves may opt for solid doors. That way everything is kept clean, no matter how long it sits unused. Solid doors also make for a visually cohesive kitchen, and you don't need to worry about keeping the contents of your shelves tidy.

Drawers are a second form of closed storage. "If I were designing a new kitchen, I'd eliminate lower cabinets altogether and just use drawers," says professional organizer Monica Ricci. "We're all so used to seeing cabinet doors in kitchens, but to make them more functional we add sliding drawers behind them. So instead of cabinets, why not just install a series of drawers in various widths and depths?"

There is also the middle ground of having mostly closed storage but leaving a few open shelves for the display of collections, or putting glass doors on some but not all of the cabinets. Large kitchens with all closed storage and lots of cabinets can have a heavy-handed look, especially if there is no break in the solid wood fronts. Ask your cabinetmaker to show you some glass options for cabinet doors. Usually you will have a choice of clear, cloudy, or wavy. Or opt for decorative carved or etched glass, stained glass, or resin panels that are colored or textured. Some resin panels even contain shells, recycled glass, or grasses that can become a main design feature of the kitchen, all the while obscuring what's behind the closed doors.

Incorporating Small-Appliance Garages

Another consideration when you are designing new cabinets is whether to include an appliance garage. Upper cabinets that sit on top of countertops present a good opportunity to hide the blender or the food processor behind a door; the appliance can then be slid forward when it is needed. When stored in lower cabinets, small appliances must be lifted and moved to the work space, which can be tough for people with limited strength or bad backs. Those who want to limit countertop clutter but can't lift a stand mixer sometimes opt for a shelf with a heavy-duty lift mechanism. The shelf holding the small appliance is stored in a base cabinet, but the whole assembly can be raised to countertop height.

An appliance garage hides the mixer when it's not in use.

PROFESSIONAL ORGANIZER
SYLVIA BORCHERT ON

Buying What You Need

I worked as a chef before I became an organizer and I always tell my clients not to buy specialty appliances, because they end up in the back of the cabinet. Buy the best you can afford of the basic things—the best knives, the best standing mixer with attachments. But don't buy sets of pots and pans. Decide on the two or three you always use and buy the best versions of those few that you can afford at the time.

Chapter 3

Bathrooms

Particularly in small or shared bathrooms, organization is key. As we're rushing to get ready in the morning, being stalled searching for makeup or sunblock can create additional stress. At night, we all want to come home to a bathroom that's clean and spa-like to wind down after a long day. Many of the solutions discussed for kitchens work every bit as well for bathrooms too, so think about your precise storage needs in this room before worrying too much about bringing in specialized organizing products or furnishings.

Woven baskets hold up well in bathrooms and are excellent at keeping small items organized.

Has your bathroom become a place where toiletries go to die? Over the years we can amass an impressive array of personal-care products, makeup, hair accessories, jewelry, medicine, and linens. Chances are, you are storing a lot of these things that you no longer use. So, start by cleaning out your vanity before looking for ways to make things more accessible.

Check for medicine and personal-care products that have passed their expiration dates. Once opened, makeup has a shelf life of about one year before bacteria accumulates that can make it unhealthful to use. Mascara should be replaced every three months, and products made with natural ingredients or without preservatives should be discarded more regularly than conventional brands. "This is really a health and safety issue. People should label their makeup products so they know when they first opened them, and make time every year to purge old products you don't use all the time," says professional organizer Sara Eizen. Dump contents of bottles into a sealed disposable container (not down the drain), and recycle the bottles. Anything toxic—like nail polish remover and some medications—should be taken to a hazardous-waste facility.

Lessons Learned from the Kitchen

Sort what you have left into groups, either by size or by category. You probably have a lot of small bottles, containers, and hair accessories that tend to float around. Small items are best stored in drawers with dividers, just as in the kitchen. Configure your drawers so that like items stay together, and use dividers or small boxes to contain them.

Cabinets with deep shelves tend to get messy quickly. Determine the sizes of items you'll be storing on shelves and consider installing some of the same pullout shelves or wire baskets that are sold for use in the kitchen. Just like the kitchen sink, the bathroom sink has pipes underneath that present an obstacle. A pullout wire basket that wraps around the pipes can make great use of the space. Or get a freestanding wicker basket with sturdy sides the same size as the shelf and angle it under the drainpipe's P-trap. Store items in the basket, then tilt it up slightly when you need to pull it forward to access what's trapped in the back.

OPPOSITE PAGE A shallow ledge behind the sinks holds small toiletries, while baskets under the console vanity keep larger items neat and contained.

TOP RIGHT It's a universal organizing principle: Label your shelves. Things just tend to stay neater that way, and everyone can pitch in when it's time to tidy up.

BOTTOM RIGHT As in the kitchen, drawer dividers keep small things organized. Choose compartment sizes based on how much makeup you need to store.

Buying New Cabinets

Plans to remodel the bathroom may point you in the direction of a new vanity. Stock vanities found at home improvement centers generally come in standard sizes of 32 inches tall and 18 to 21 inches deep. Cabinets sold specifically as vanities often have pull-out side shelves where you can store narrow bottles. Semicustom cabinets will offer more storage hardware choices than stock, but the style and color will still need to be selected from a catalog of standard offerings. Depending on the size of your bathroom and your storage needs, you may get the most for your money with custom cabinets. That way you aren't limited to basic styles and you can get the height, depth, and storage solutions that really suit your needs.

INTERIOR DESIGNER
KIT DAVEY ON

Sharing a Bathroom

You need to be even more organized when four or five people share the same bathroom. I tell my clients to work out a time schedule and post it on the front and back of the door. Rotate every couple of months so that the last person doesn't always get cold water, and make sure you have a clock in the bathroom. To keep the countertop uncluttered, each person should have their own caddy that's stored in the cabinet. During their bathroom time, they have all their own toiletries on the counter and then put everything back in the caddy to be stored when they leave.

TOP Use travel bags year-round to stay organized.

BOTTOM A wire basket can contain one person's toiletries in the shower.

RIGHT An off-the-shelf vanity and matching tower from Pottery Barn provide plenty of personalized storage space.

Freestanding Furniture

A low dresser on wheels provides flexibility and extra counter space. The collection of stacked baskets makes the most of an awkward corner, and a repurposed ladder provides lots of extra space for hanging towels.

Small bathrooms with pedestal or wall-mount sinks can benefit from a piece of freestanding furniture. Even bathrooms with built-in cabinetry often need additional storage space. Look for tall, narrow, and shallow dressers if you need more drawers for toiletries. There are also specialized cabinets meant to fit around the toilet tank that can match the style of your built-in cabinetry and store extra paper products or linens.

A bench next to the tub is useful for helping a child during bath time. Put baskets underneath the bench for bath toys or extra towels. Small bookshelves also can be repurposed for the bathroom. Open shelves display, rather than hide, so they are best used for folded and stacked towels that look good together, or glass bottles of bath salts and soaps that are pretty and practical.

Dressing Areas

A small, low desk turns a bathroom into a full-service dressing area. Install a mirror on the wall behind the vanity and light it from the sides instead of from above to get a realistic picture of what you'll look like when you leave the bathroom. Makeup vanities with one or more small drawers will keep everything you need close at hand. A small padded stool on wheels should be sized to slide under the vanity when not in use. Keep the top of the vanity from becoming too cluttered by using small, lidded containers for swabs and cotton balls, and glass cylinders for makeup brushes. Men can benefit from a small desk as well—it comes in handy for shaving with an electric razor, applying sunblock, or styling hair while the sink area is in use by someone else.

ABOVE Dressing tables should be lower than the vanity so they are a comfortable height for sitting. This example has a hutch on top for extra storage.

RIGHT Shelves made of teak slats are ideal for bathrooms, because teak is naturally resistant to the moisture of this wet environment.

POTTERY BARN CREATIVE DIRECTOR
CELIA TEJADA ON

Going Vertical

Simple freestanding towers with baskets that fit well on each shelf maximize floor space. Personalize the baskets with different colored liners or monogrammed liners. I also love hooks in a bathroom. Who has time to fold towels? It's a creative way to see things and still keep them looking organized.

Toiletries and Towels

A fixture with a shelf, rack, and hooks gives you options for storing and drying a large number of towels.

Just about everything that needs to be stored in the bathroom is small, and some things like hairpins and tweezers can be nearly impossible to find if you don't keep them in a predictable spot. A number of the organizers on our design panel suggested that each person in the family should have his or her own designated shelf or drawer in a shared bathroom. This is more efficient and helps keep the space tidy. Read on for other ideas on organizing toiletries and linens.

Shelves

There is usually a fair amount of open space midway up the wall in bathrooms. Look for areas above or next to the vanity or above the toilet to install a single shelf or group of shelves. Shallow shelves that can hold one row of toiletries or boxes of accessories will have a cleaner look than deep shelves where things tend to get lost in the back. Stick to short shelf lengths and pay attention to weight loads if you plan to put anything heavy on them. Solid glass or wood shelves are a better choice than slatted or wire shelving for small items, as things won't fall through the cracks. Moreover, if a bottle leaks, its contents won't be as likely to run down the wall onto the floor. Deeper slatted shelves are great for folded towels, as they allow more air circulation.

Hooks

Hung individually or in a row, wall hooks can hold more than just towels. Put them on the back of the bathroom door to hang-dry laundry or your outfit for the day. Hang loofahs and scrubbers next to the bathtub. Small hooks over the vanity can corral hair accessories.

Children love to organize when given the right tools. Install hooks just above head height and encourage them to hang their own towels, clothes, and mesh bags of bath toys. To avoid accidents, move the hooks up the wall as the child grows.

Towel Racks

A long rack allows towels to dry faster than a hook. Because people tend to hang multiple wet towels on a single rack, it's important to anchor racks into the wall studs for solid support. Select a finish that coordinates with fixtures in the room, or use a found object such as a repurposed curtain rod. A heated towel rack will have the dual benefits of warming the room and drying towels faster. Some heated racks hang from the wall, while others come up from the floor, depending on where the natural-gas source or electrical receptacle is located.

ABOVE Leave a little open space, select a harmonious palette, and intersperse an attractive bottle or rolls of paper among your linens to create little vignettes on each shelf.

RIGHT If you want to use all the same color towels in a shared bath, monogram them with initials or numbers.

PROFESSIONAL ORGANIZER
SYLVIA BORCHERT ON

Towels

Racks allow for the most air movement and, thus, keep thick towels from being wet so long that they start to get smelly. Install towel racks at different heights for each member of the family and have each person select a coordinating towel color for bath, hand, and washcloths so you know whose is whose. Try varying shades of the same color for a harmonious look.

Baskets

Woven baskets have an earthy, natural look and hold up well in humid environments, making them ideal for bathroom storage. Put two baskets with lids under a pedestal or hanging sink to store toiletries and hide them from view. Put one next to the tub with a stack of fresh linens so people can grab them as needed. A large lidded basket can act as a bench while adding storage capacity.

If you opt for metal baskets, be sure they are suitable for wet areas so they don't leave rust stains on the floor or the tub. Plastic buckets are foolproof, but some types can emit gases; opt for a bucket that you know is made of an inert plastic that can eventually be recycled.

Recessed Shelves

Wall niches or recessed shelves allow you to utilize the space within walls. Most homes have 4-inch-deep, 14- to 22-inch-wide cavities between the wall studs. Cut away the drywall and you can access that area for shelving that does not protrude into the room. Because the shelves are so shallow, they're best used to display decorative items. In showers they're the perfect size for shampoo and conditioner bottles. To really make them blend into their surroundings, match the sides and back of the niche with the same tiles or paint color used on the wall.

Medicine Cabinets

Not every bathroom needs a medicine cabinet, but if you are short on storage space, it's a great way to get two uses out of the vanity mirror. These cabinets can be recessed slightly into the wall, or hung on the surface. Choose one that matches the style of your vanity or that looks like no more than a mirror. You can also find wall-mount cabinets without mirrors that hang on a wall and have glass doors. These work well for displaying perfume bottles and decorative soaps.

TOP LEFT A trio of artistic baskets warm up the bathroom and also contain extra clean towels.

MIDDLE LEFT Recessed shelves placed across from the showerhead keep toiletries dry but within reach.

BOTTOM LEFT Behind the bathroom door is a perfect place for a cabinet of recessed shelves, just deep enough to hold one row of shampoo bottles or nail polish.

PROFESSIONAL ORGANIZER
JEN M. R. DOMAN ON

Medicine in the Bathroom

Despite the name, medications really should not be stored in a medicine cabinet. The heat generated from lights around the medicine cabinet and the daily shower steam essentially cook the chemicals at a low temperature over time, reducing the effectiveness of the medication. Instead, put medications in a kitchen drawer that isn't near the stove, or keep them in the refrigerator. Now you have more storage space in the bathroom!

Reclaimed Douglas fir was used to make this custom vanity and simple recessed medicine cabinet with a frameless mirror.

Laundry and Trash

Solid lidded trash cans hide messes, protect the floor underneath, and block odors.

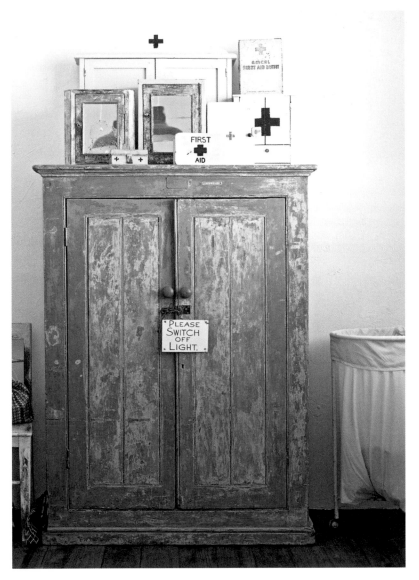

M ost bathrooms don't have space for a laundry basket. If yours does, however, it's a good idea to add one so you don't wind up gathering a pile of discarded clothes from the floor every day. The type of basket you need depends on how dirty the clothes get in your household. "Woven baskets and cloth containers allow dirty clothes to breathe. But if those clothes belong to a child who is on four sports teams, you don't want to smell them for the few days they might sit, waiting for the laundry to be done," says professional organizer Jen M. R. Doman. "In that case, a lidded metal or plastic container is best." When clothes aren't that soiled, a stack of metal bins or baskets with wide-mouthed openings give people the chance to sort whites, darks, and dry cleaning at the source.

Bathroom trash cans should be conveniently situated near the sink and toilet. If you can spare the storage space, hiding the trash can in the cabinet under the sink prevents pets and toddlers from getting into it. There are also small metal cans with foot controls for opening the lid. Avoid using baskets as trash cans in bathrooms; a leaky bottle can stain the floor tile underneath the basket without your being aware of it.

ABOVE LEFT Laundry baskets on wheels can be rolled over to the washing machine when full. This bathroom's antique dresser also provides a surface to display a collection of tin first aid boxes.

ABOVE RIGHT A wicker basket placed between the shower and sink encourages people to deposit dirty towels rather than drop them on the floor.

Tub and Shower Areas

A heated towel rack and a pedestal just outside the shower door keep fresh towels close at hand.

If you aren't vigilant, the areas around bathtubs and showers can easily become cluttered with hair products, soaps, razors, and the like. The narrow ledge around the tub gets jammed to the limit, and things get harder to find—not to mention that it makes the tub difficult to enter and exit without knocking something over. Adding a shelf above the level where the shower water hits the wall will keep things clean and organized. If adding a shelf is not an option, hang a shower caddy over the showerhead or straddle a bath caddy across the tub to keep the essentials near at hand.

Be sure there's a place to hang at least the towel you are about to use, right outside the shower or bath. Two hooks—one for a towel and one for a bathrobe—are even better. For freestanding tubs, a small table or chair is a perfect spot to set a book and a cup of tea. Drop-in or under-mount tubs can have deep ledges, and it's too tempting to keep all your bottles there. Try to limit this to just what you use on a daily basis and group the bottles in an old milk-jar holder to keep them looking neat. Put the bar of soap in a soap holder so it doesn't slide off the edge when wet. Instead of keeping bath salts and soaps in the containers in which you purchased them, transfer them to glass canisters and add a few water-loving indoor plants to create a spa-like feel while you're bathing.

PROFESSIONAL ORGANIZER MONICA RICCI ON

Corralling Clutter

Try to limit the number of hair and body products you have open at any one time, and get rid of things you opened but no longer use. If you must have lots of bottles open at once in shared bathrooms, get a multitiered spring tension rod—a vertical pole with shelves that extends floor to ceiling—for the corner of the shower and give each person his or her own shelf. Then you won't be tripping over bottles around the tub or shower.

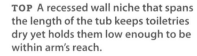

TOP A recessed wall niche that spans the length of the tub keeps toiletries dry yet holds them low enough to be within arm's reach.

BOTTOM LEFT Seashells in glass apothecary jars perched on the tub surround are a daily reminder of last summer's vacation.

BOTTOM RIGHT Metal shower caddies hold your most often used toiletries and can also have places for washcloths and soap.

Chapter 4

Family and Dining Rooms

Aside from the kitchen, family rooms and dining rooms are the parts of the house that see the most action and need to accommodate the widest range of activities. They are the places where we entertain guests, where kids play or do homework, where we gather to watch movies and listen to music, and where we relax at the end of the day. If these rooms are cluttered, they are neither ready to receive guests nor very satisfactory as places to unwind. This chapter explores the best ways to get things under control, to organize your bookshelves, to display photos and collections, and to make better use of an underutilized formal living room.

Freestanding cabinets
help keep living spaces
uncluttered while
providing needed
storage.

Gathering Areas

Living rooms, family rooms, great rooms—whatever you call them, these are a home's public spaces. They are the places where people gather to entertain guests, watch television, play games, curl up on the couch with a book or a laptop, or simply to be together. Many homes no longer have a formal living room, and in those that do, the owners often choose to turn them into functional, multipurpose rooms rather than save them for company. It's always the best idea to look at a home's layout creatively: Make the rooms functional for what you actually do rather than for the purpose the builder had in mind. Perhaps the dining room should be turned into a family room so you can keep an eye on the kids from the kitchen. Or perhaps the living room might make more sense as a home office.

Interior designer Kit Davey suggests turning large gathering spaces like great rooms into zones. "Arrange the furniture so that you have a television zone, an eating zone, a music area, a play area—whatever makes sense for your family." Davey points out that a large space broken up this way tends to make more visual sense and to be less intimidating to plan because you can do it in stages.

Small-Space Living

Most often the problem isn't too much space but too little. When you have a single room that needs to work as the gathering area for an entire family, it can get cluttered quickly with everybody's things. Keep shoes, coats, and backpacks out of these rooms by having a place for them near the entry door (see chapter 8). Use end tables or a fireplace hearth for artistic display and keep the coffee table clear so people have a space to set a drink or to lay out a game. Baskets under tables can corral toys and blankets. You may even want to look for a coffee table that can accommodate baskets underneath or one that opens like a chest. Professional organizer Monica Ricci is a big fan of storage ottomans. "In a small space, these are great multipurpose pieces. I use them to store board games, extra blankets, toys, or video games," Ricci says.

OPPOSITE PAGE Keeping surfaces uncluttered is easier if you have space under tables to store toys, games, and blankets.

TOP LEFT This freestanding cabinet creates a visual separation between the entryway and living space. It provides a large amount of closed storage to keep the room uncluttered.

TOP RIGHT Low cushions around the coffee table create a comfortable space for playing games.

BOTTOM A narrow bench behind the sofa keeps favorite items close at hand but hidden from the conversation area.

Off-the-shelf storage systems are available for a variety of multimedia needs. This bank of modular drawers and shelves has a narrow slot under the television for DVD players and cable boxes.

POTTERY BARN CREATIVE DIRECTOR
CELIA TEJADA ON

Charging Stations

Charging stations manage all the cables and give you a place to put cell phones, cameras, and Bluetooth devices so you don't lose any of your gadgets and you know they're charged and ready to go each morning. I recommend putting one in the room you're in most often—be it the living room or the kitchen—one in the bedroom, and one at the front door, if that's not near the living space.

Organizing Audio and Video Equipment

Even a few years ago, keeping all of your music, movies, video games, and the devices used to play them could be quite a challenge. We made room for large armoires to hold television sets, CD players, and stereo systems. We bought towers to store CD and DVD cases. So much has changed! Today, most new televisions are narrow enough to hang on the wall or to rest on a shallow table. They have become less obtrusive. New music and movie purchases are now frequently downloaded to computers or iPods, making storage for CDs a thing of the past.

Going Digital

If you still have a collection of CDs and DVDs taking up space in your living room, think about recycling the cases and putting the disks in sleeves. The sleeves can then be kept in cases sold for that purpose, or in three-ring binders organized by genre. Put a label on the spine and set it on a bookshelf; it will take up less space than a dictionary. Professional organizer Jen M. R. Doman encourages her clients to go digital from now on and to replace existing collections with downloadable versions. "This is one of those projects that you may never find time to do, so I suggest hiring a high school student for the job. In about a quarter of the time it might take you to do it, they can digitally re-create your music and movie collection, and in the process free up so much space in the home," Doman says. If you have old cassette tapes you can't bear to part with, have the contents transferred to CDs. They will last longer and be easier to store.

Shrinking Equipment

In many homes, iPod docking stations have taken the place of multibox stereos and speakers. You may need to find a place for only a DVD player, a DVR, and a cable box. Even this equipment is shrinking in size. Game systems can be combined with DVD players, and if you have cable and a DVR, they're usually housed in a single box. But whether you're playing high-tech catch-up or you're already taking advantage of every new digital option, the amount of media equipment you actually need to store these days can often be housed in a small cabinet under the television. If the TV hangs on an interior wall, you may be able to claim some closet space in an adjoining room for the DVD player and the cable box. Wherever you put this equipment, make sure it's well ventilated, as high temperatures tend to shorten the shelf life of such machines.

Thin, stand-alone televisions, either hanging on a wall or sitting on a table, have become more like another piece of art in living rooms.

A multipurpose built-in can be an effective organizing tool for small homes and living rooms without formal entryways. Mail and items needing to be sorted are in metal baskets, and toys are hidden in closed cabinets.

Organizing Games and Toys

Whether your household includes toddlers with small toys, kids with puzzles and video games, or just adults who like to play Scrabble after dinner and host the occasional game night, most people have games and toys to be stored. Depending on the size of your collection, you may find space in the living room itself, or you may have to explore other solutions, such as a corner of the entryway closet, a cabinet in the garage, or excess space in a dining room buffet.

When you have a small collection of frequently used games, keep all the pieces in their original boxes and put the boxes in a lidded basket, along with scoring pads and pencils. That basket can then be used as an end table in the living room or stowed under a desk. Interior designer Kit Davey recommends sorting through your games once a year and getting rid of what you no longer use. "Swap the games you're tired of with friends. And give away all your old puzzles. Don't store puzzles—once you have put them together, you'll probably never do them again," Davey advises.

Kids' toys should be kept accessible and as organized as possible. Baskets and bins are great for toys with small pieces and can be stored on shelves or under coffee tables or end tables. Line the baskets or bins with different colored fabrics so you can teach the children to put their toys away by group—all the blocks in one, all the cars in another. This will make them easier to find. Anything that requires adult supervision can be stored higher up in a closet or on a bookshelf.

Musical Instruments

Pianos are frequently part of the living room, and when there are multiple players, it makes sense to have a system in place for organizing everyone's music. Piano benches usually have built-in storage. Instead of simply stowing all the sheet music in the bench, however, it can help to put the music in a three-ring binder, using tabs to organize by composer or genre. Each child who is taking piano lessons should have his or her own binder; these can be kept in the kids' bedrooms if the bench doesn't have sufficient space. For guitars, cellos, flutes, and other more movable instruments, a filing box with handles will keep the sheet music organized and is easy to transport. You may also want to use an instrument stand so you can display the instrument when it's not in use and keep it off the floor.

Lightweight metal baskets with handles keep small toys organized. These are the perfect depth for a standard bookshelf.

PROFESSIONAL ORGANIZER
JEN M. R. DOMAN ON

Getting Kids Involved

Parents sometimes don't have a good sense of which toys and games are still being used on a regular basis, so it's best to get the kids involved in the storage solution. Have them create a hierarchy of which games should be higher or lower on the shelf, and make sure they can reach the ones they use most often. This creates a level of independence, and it can also be a good opportunity to teach the concept of charity. Once they decide which toys they no longer want, take them to a local children's hospital and have them give the toys away.

LEFT A round woven basket keeps a small supply of firewood at hand, while a metal stand corrals the fireplace tools.

BELOW Cut flowers bring a taste of the garden into the living room. An etched glass frame reflects the green pottery in the foreground.

OPPOSITE PAGE, TOP LEFT Fill the inside of a fireplace no longer in use with an artfully composed stack of cut wood, ends facing out.

OPPOSITE PAGE, TOP RIGHT Collections of baskets, small statues, decorative eggs, and wooden spoons surround a fireplace with Spanish ceramic tiles.

OPPOSITE PAGE, BOTTOM Two windows and benches with storage drawers flank the gas fireplace. Above, a single painting leans casually against a faux-painted wall.

Around the Fireplace

Fireplace mantels should be used for display, not for stacks of mail or whatever else people carry through the door. Making space elsewhere for the usual things you stash on the mantel should put an end to this practice. To decorate simply, select a few of your favorite items that have some similarities in color or style, then create a vignette. Wood-burning fireplaces that are no longer in use can be treated like a picture frame for decorative objects. For fireplaces that are in use, have a dedicated container with enough wood for a single fire and store the rest outside.

Displaying Collections

Even if you don't regard yourself as a collector, chances are you have at least a handful of decorative objects that you want to display, and doing so effectively takes a bit of thought. "A collection doesn't necessarily mean a grouping of fine or expensive things. It's simply three or more of anything," says interior designer Kit Davey. "Group them together and find a platform to display them on. Arrange them in odd numbers, and put some air between groupings."

Less Is More

There's a fine line between clutter and the artful display of a collection. "Smaller groups are more impactful than having a wall full of various items," says professional organizer Monica Ricci. "The trick is to keep it small and concentrated. If you spread everything around, it will start to look messy." Stick to one collection per room, or a few small, grouped collections in each space.

When you're starting with dozens of items, select the ones you really love or those that have sentimental value. You can always rotate new items in every few months, or with the seasons, so that all of your favorites make an appearance at some point during the year. Not seeing everything all at once will make you appreciate each piece even more.

LEFT Your eye can easily find the various groupings of glass and pottery because the shelves are kept sparse and are punctuated with stacks of books interspersed among the collections.

ABOVE Items with no discernable connection can somehow look just right grouped together when they are all of a similar color.

BELOW LEFT Small prints arranged in three rows of three make a strong statement at less cost than a single large piece of art.

BELOW RIGHT Shallow boxes keep a collection of butterflies anchored on a shelf. They are also easy to move without damaging the delicate contents.

DESIGN CONSULTANT
KATE PARKER ON

Keeping to a Theme

Particularly when you don't live in a large space, it's best to build collections in one theme or color palette. Say you've always been drawn to elephants: When you bring home your latest elephant figurine or picture, you can add it to the rest of your collection and still have an organized look. But if you collect too many different types of things, it will quickly look disheveled.

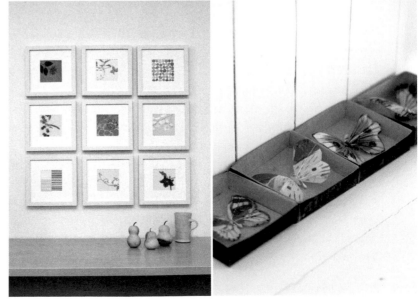

Staying Clean and Keeping Put

Arranging decorative items on a surface means a bit more dusting each week, but once you have edited your display, it will be worth the extra effort to keep it clean. However, if the dusting doesn't always get done in your home, or if your collection has lots of small parts that are difficult to keep clean, consider displaying the collection inside Lucite boxes.

"I love to put small collections in a wall niche behind an interesting clear panel and backlight the items," says interior designer Lori Dennis. "Or you can put vases or figurines in Lucite boxes, which can then be either stacked one on top of the other or propped up on squares or skinny posts to make the display three dimensional. You'll be creating a museum-quality presentation of your own personal style."

Once you get everything the way you want it, take extra precautions to keep your things safe. Professional organizer Deborah Silberberg uses clear museum wax to affix breakable items to shelves. "You can use dental floss to remove the wax from the collectible later on. This keeps everything in place, even if there's an earthquake or the kids run down the stairs," Silberberg observes.

ABOVE LEFT Museum-quality displays are a cinch to create with store-bought shadow boxes. An added bonus: You'll never have to dust the collections!

ABOVE RIGHT This living room combines collectibles of different styles and eras. On the mantel, three balls of vintage string and a grouping of busts are bookended by 19th-century candelabras.

RIGHT Lucite boxes keep treasured or rare collections safe and maintenance-free.

Take boxes in different shapes and sizes, stack them in alternating directions, then create small vignettes in each opening.

Bookshelves

Organized bookshelves are visually pleasing and will also make it easier to find what you're looking for.

When you're in the market for bookshelves, think about what you want to store on them before making the purchase. Shelf spans should be sized according to the weight of what they will hold. Buy solid wood bookshelves if you can; those made of particleboard are more apt to sag over time, particularly if the shelf spans are longer than 3 feet. Used bookshelves are generally easy to find, and refurbishing them with a fresh coat of paint or stain is no more than a weekend project.

Purging

The most common mistake made with bookshelves is to pack them with books and nothing else. This is fine in a library, but it can make a living space look heavy and disheveled. If you have a bookshelf in need of a facelift, start by emptying the shelves. Interior designer Kit Davey tells her clients that they need to remove between a quarter and a third of the books to allow for air space and accessories. Be realistic about the books you want to keep. Put them in stacks: books you plan to read, favorites you keep coming back to, reference books, and books you will probably never open again. Those you can't see reading again should be donated to your local public library or, if they are paperbacks in poor condition, recycled. Things with sentimental value—old yearbooks, for instance, or childhood storybooks that you haven't looked at in years—can be preserved in closed storage in the attic or garage.

Once you've removed what you don't need on display, there are a variety of ways to make books look attractive on their shelves. You can stack them by spine color, by subject, or by size. Design consultant Kate Parker always takes the dust jackets off books when she designs a bookshelf. "It gives the books that instant vintage feel," Parker says.

ABOVE LEFT Leaning bookshelves are deep at the bottom and shallow up top. Their ladder shapes, with open sides and backs, make them visually recess into the wall.

ABOVE RIGHT Corner racks create an orderly tower of books and take up minimal space on the floor.

Adding Style and Dimension

Now it's time for the fun part. Place each stack of books back on the shelves, keeping them in the order you have chosen. Vary the stacking techniques on each shelf if you can. On one shelf, stand books with spines facing out and use short stacks of horizontal books as bookends. On another, fill the shelf with books of the same height or color and leave space in the middle or on either side for a vase or framed picture. "Stick to three or four stacking techniques and repeat them throughout, occasionally standing back to make sure you have the right balance," Kit Davey recommends.

Bookshelves with multiple dividers are easier to design than those with long, uninterrupted spans of shelving. For the latter, create mini-groupings on each shelf with objects placed between varying stacks of books. When you do have smaller squares to work with, think of each opening as a frame in which to create a unique vignette.

INTERIOR DESIGNER
KIT DAVEY ON

Accessorizing Shelves

The openings between groupings of books are ideal for display. Go on a treasure hunt throughout your home looking for objects which reflect the feel, theme, and color scheme of the room—teapots, vases, sculpture, musical instruments, boxes, baskets, pottery, framed art, or photographs all can work. But don't clutter the space with too many things. A few truly beautiful objects that have meaning for you will be most impactful.

OPPOSITE PAGE, TOP LEFT Painted and stacked wooden crates are transformed into an inexpensive bookshelf. Each cubby is the perfect size for a vignette of books and art.

OPPOSITE PAGE, TOP RIGHT Instead of piling books and magazines all the way to the top, leave a little space and set a ceramic pot or a framed picture here and there.

OPPOSITE PAGE, BOTTOM Magazine and book spines grouped by color create a visual frame around a piece of art hung on the face of the shelves.

RIGHT Mixing short and tall shelves breaks up the expanse of a floor-to-ceiling built-in. Metal numbers that function as bookends on four shelves draw your eye.

Dining Rooms

L arge families and people who regularly host dinner parties will get a lot of use out of a dining room with a table that seats eight or ten people. Wall space in a dining room is often used for displaying photos or collections, but it also may be needed for a cabinet or hutch that you use for storing the dishes and crockery that come out only on special occasions.

Displaying China

If the cabinets in your dining room are stuffed to the brim, spend a Saturday taking everything out; then you can start over. Decide what really needs to be there. Large sets of china that are rarely used may need to be stored elsewhere, particularly if there is not room in the kitchen for all the things in day-to-day circulation. Select a few family heirlooms and a grouping of platters—or a creamer and sugar bowl from your grand-mother's china set—and put them in the glass hutch above the cabinet. Or hang a selection of plates on the wall so you can enjoy seeing them. What you rarely use can be stored in zippered cozies and boxes divided for storing glasses. Wrap things carefully and store them in the garage so that your dining room hutch looks less cluttered and your best pieces are visible. For the things you want to display, follow the same techniques described for bookshelves: combining dishes, framed photographs, and objects collected over the years to create eye-pleasing vignettes.

OPPOSITE PAGE Display dishes standing up on shallow shelves and hang teacups from hooks on the lips of the shelves. A collection of pots is put to good use as planters.

TOP LEFT To create hidden storage areas, cover glass doors with your favorite wallpaper or sew short curtains to stretch across open shelves of a cabinet.

TOP RIGHT Dark book-shelves lining the walls of this dining room turn it into a homey study. Crown molding gives the shelves a built-in look.

BOTTOM Thin out large collections of pottery and display your favorite pieces on open dining room shelves so you can enjoy seeing them every day.

Multipurpose Dining Rooms

Even if you use your dining room regularly for family gatherings, there are lots of times when the room is unoccupied. Particularly in smaller homes, this space can be put to additional use as a work area for kids or adults.

Professional organizer Monica Ricci turns a dining room buffet into a mini office. "Take the bottom half of the buffet and use it to store an open-top file box for bills," she advises. "Keep a laptop, checkbooks, mailing supplies and pens in one of the top drawers. Then you'll have a little bill-paying station in the dining room and can use the table to get the work done."

Sara Eizen suggests using the room as a crafts area for kids. "Allot part of the buffet cabinet for art supplies and a roll of brown craft paper. Roll the paper out onto the dining room table to protect it, then let the kids use their coloring books or create art projects," Eizen recommends. You might also have space to store gift wrapping supplies, such as bags, paper, and ribbon. The large dining room table is an excellent work space for such tasks.

ABOVE LEFT Place an armchair in a corner of the dining room to create a quiet spot for reading or talking on the phone.

ABOVE RIGHT Narrow drawers are ideal for keeping small art supplies organized. A rustic wooden table and easy-to-clean metal chairs make this dining room a favorite spot for crafts projects.

OPPOSITE PAGE This built-in china cabinet includes a pullout writing surface, integral lights, and a phone jack for a mini office.

INTERIOR DESIGNER
LORI DENNIS ON

Combination Dining and Reading Rooms

One of my favorite things to do is line the walls of a dining room with bookshelves. I create built-in benches beneath windows for added closed storage and have cushions made for the tops. It becomes a little nook where you can sit and read—a great way to use a quiet room for storage, reading, and resting.

Displaying Photos

In a room with white walls and furniture, white frames and mats make the photos pop.

With digital cameras, families tend to have hundreds, if not thousands, of pictures stored efficiently on their computers. But most of us still like to print our best shots and use them to decorate the walls so family and friends can admire them. In fact, digital cameras give even beginning photographers the ability to produce truly artistic images that can be cropped, enlarged, and touched up for red-eye so that they are worthy of that top spot on the wall.

The Creative Method

We may be equipped to take better pictures, but many of us are less confident when it comes to displaying the results. Pottery Barn creative director Celia Tejada offers a wealth of ideas on that process. "Putting together a grouping of photography to hang on the wall is one of my passions," she says. Following her approach will ensure a great result.

First, she suggests selecting a frame profile that blends well with the architectural style of your home. If you have white trim and doors, pick a white painted frame with a profile that mimics the molding style used around the house. If you have dark wood, pick a mahogany or espresso finished frame. For an 8-by-10-foot wall, buy 10 frames. Get four of one size, two of another, one very large frame, and three in other miscellaneous sizes.

For a cohesive arrangement, it's best to go with either all color or all black-and-white photographs. Choose one or two images that you love and have them blown up to fit the larger frames. "Something that can be cropped for maximum impact would be perfect," Tejada says. Then take your favorite photo or group of photos and hang those first in the center of the wall. Hang the other images around them to make your own art gallery. "Basically by using the same profile and color frames in multiple sizes, you can't go wrong. From there, the sky is the limit," Tejada says. "Clip butterflies to the edges of frames, print quotes and place them in some of the frames, and add flea market finds to the edges of others to give them character. Or buy one elaborate frame and put it in the mix. There are many ways to get creative once you have the basics down."

ABOVE LEFT The wall at the end of a stairway is generally open space, perfect for an artistic grouping of photos.

ABOVE RIGHT A small arrangement of photos over an open console is bookended by faux deer heads that visually contain the art on a large wall.

The Foolproof Method

The instructions on the previous page provide a variety of ideas for the style and composition of your display, but you do still have to measure and make sure each frame is level and evenly spaced. If this is not something you feel confident about, there are more straightforward ways to approach the process. Professional organizer Sara Eizen suggests templates to her clients (see Resources). You decide on a grouping of picture frames and buy a paper template that shows you exactly where to drive each nail for a balanced, level arrangement. This way, you don't even need a tape measure.

Professional organizer Sylvia Borchert points out that you can do much the same thing on your own with a large roll of craft paper. "Roll out a piece of paper on the floor that's the same size as the area you want to cover on the wall. Then place each frame on the paper and try different configurations until you're happy with one. Outline each frame on the paper, then tape the paper on the wall and drive the nails," Borchert says. "Once all the nails are up, you tear off the paper and can hang the frames." If you make the frame outlines level on the paper when it's on the ground, and make the paper level when you hang it on the wall, the frames will be level when you hang them.

The Leaning Method

For an easy-to-change display that doesn't involve touching up the walls later on, install shallow shelves on a wall and use them to support your pictures and art. You might select a range of frame sizes and shapes, but stick to one frame color or finish. Or you may want to go for a more eclectic look in which you vary the color but stick to a single size of frame. Layer smaller frames over large ones and add a vase with flowers or a few candles to the mix.

OPPOSITE PAGE, TOP For something entirely different, take your display off the wall altogether. There are many hanging clip systems on the market that turn your pictures into a free-floating mobile.

OPPOSITE PAGE, BOTTOM Pre-designed templates are one easy way to create a dynamic arrangement within a set area.

RIGHT Keeping picture displays looking fresh is easy with shelves. Move the frames around every few months and change out the accessories to add color or seasonal decoration.

Chapter 5

Bedrooms

A cluttered bedroom is anything but the restful place you want to come home to after a long day. This chapter focuses on ways to get organized in every bedroom in your home—including nurseries and kids' rooms, where the multitude of small belongings require unique solutions; guest bedrooms, where your everyday activities need to make way for the occasional visitor; and master bedrooms, where the goal should be to keep away anything that distracts you from the most restful endeavors. In the end, you can have systems in place to keep the bedroom peaceful.

When space is tight,
creative storage
solutions make all
the difference.

Personal Retreats

One shallow shelf above the bed keeps books close at hand while limiting the number you keep in the bedroom.

In small homes, the master bedroom sometimes has to fight for its independence. After you fit in a bed, night tables, and a dresser, it's tough to resist the impulse to also squeeze in a work space and an exercise machine when there's no better place in the house for them. Resist the temptation!

Master bedrooms should be kept serene and uncluttered. If you have a desk for work in the room, no matter how organized you keep it, you will probably feel its presence while you're attempting to fall asleep. Likewise, exercise equipment will probably just remind you of the workouts you skipped, while attracting piles of discarded clothes. When you don't allow such makeshift hanging places in the room, you are more likely to put away the clothes where they belong. Keeping the room sparse will also be more restful and make the room more attractive.

Sounds easy, but how do you sidestep such understandable bad habits? Design consultant Kate Parker suggests making it a rule not to take your work bag, cell phone, or any business-related materials into the bedroom. "Even if you have to put a chair or a small console right outside the bedroom because there's no other great place to set these things, it's better to do that than to disrupt the peace and tranquility of your bedroom," she says. "If this is not an option, get a few baskets with lids and put these things in there so you can't see them once the lid is on."

INTERIOR DESIGNER LORI DENNIS ON

Healthful Bedrooms

Plants can improve the air quality in your home, but it's best to keep them out of the bedroom because they absorb oxygen. You wind up competing with them for oxygen as you sleep. It's probably also best to avoid having electronic equipment in the bedroom. Some people feel that electromagnetic frequencies disrupt their sleep, though others don't notice this effect.

TOP In tight quarters, use small-scale furnishings and mirrors to make the space feel brighter and airier.

BOTTOM LEFT An extra dining room chair fills in as a bedside table.

BOTTOM RIGHT An arrangement of photos and candles warms up this nightstand.

Shelves and Hooks

A few shallow shelves in the bedroom can be useful for framed photographs, scented candles, or a select group of favorite objects. Consider a continuous shelf about 14 inches below ceiling level along one wall or even around the entire room. It's a great way to display sentimental objects that you don't need to set hands on very often, or to show off a collection—hats or purses, for instance. Don't put anything heavy on shelves over the bed, however, and secure items that might break if they fell. Lower shelves, next to the bed, can hold the books and magazines you read before going to sleep. There are also hanging magazine racks covered in upholstery that are sold for this purpose.

Under-Bed Storage

When you're really pressed for storage space, the large area underneath the bed can start to look pretty appealing. Before you resort to this solution, however, consider whether there are any other places that will serve the same purpose. Professional organizer Jen M. R. Doman advises her clients not to store things under the bed if at all possible. "Basic feng shui principles say not to store

books and photos under the bed because the thoughts of books and vibes from photos permeate your psyche as you sleep," Doman says.

If you do need to use the space under the bed—and the bigger the bed, the more usable space there is—a good practice is to keep things in labeled containers. This way it doesn't become a place to stash things that you don't really even need to hold on to. Pottery Barn creative director Celia Tejada suggests using a trundle for extra bedding, because it's already contained and on wheels. There are also various lidded, shallow boxes on the market designed specifically for under-bed storage. Whether you go with boxes or baskets, lids will keep the contents free of dust. Sealed plastic containers will keep out bugs as well. Label each container on its sides so you don't have to drag it out to recall what's inside.

TOP LEFT Shallow, white floating shelves visually recede into the wall, allowing a display of family photos to shine.

MIDDLE LEFT Low, wide baskets hold extra blankets under the bed. Open baskets are best for items you use regularly.

BOTTOM LEFT A bed skirt hides a wooden drawer on wheels.

PROFESSIONAL ORGANIZER MONICA RICCI ON

Under-Bed Storage

I encourage people to buy bed frames with more than 6 or 7 inches of clearance underneath so they can fit luggage and other bulky items. If you aren't in the market for a new bed frame, consider putting your current frame on bed risers or even cinder blocks so you can fit plastic tubs or stacking drawers under the bed. Put long-term storage items under the center of the bed and things you want access to around the edges. Then get an extra-long bed skirt to hide the cinder blocks and containers.

Sturdy wooden crates
are repurposed as
a bed frame with
built-in storage.

Double-Duty Furniture

In small spaces, look for ways to get the most out of your furniture. For example, a chest at the end of the bed can store extra linens or books while also being used as a place to sit. Nightstands with drawers or cabinets don't have to contain things used only at bedtime. They can also be excellent spots for storing extra clothing or toiletries.

Professional organizer Jen M. R. Doman warns not to fill your bedroom with large furniture. "Consider the size of the room and what pieces you can use that will make it feel homey but not overbearing," Doman says. "If a piece of furniture takes up 50 percent of the wall space, it's too big." She also suggests keeping work areas small, if you must have one in the bedroom. She prefers a delicate desk at the end of the bed, with the chair facing the bed, rather than taking up wall space. The desk can then double as a dressing table.

Baskets and Boxes

As in every other room, baskets in the bedroom can be enormously useful. Stack a few lidded baskets in a corner and store seasonal clothes, hats, or scarves in them. Place a large basket at the end of the bed for extra blankets or to throw decorative pillows into every night when you climb into bed. A few small baskets on top of the dresser can contain receipts, spare change, and other items from your pockets so the surfaces don't get cluttered. Sort through the baskets every few weeks to keep them from spilling over.

Laundry

Having a designated area for dirty laundry will help avoid makeshift piles on the bedroom or bathroom floor. If you frequent the gym, a lidded, nonbreathable container will prevent odors from escaping into the room. When you have the space for two containers, or a larger container with two bags inside, you can sort lights and darks as you throw dirty clothes into the hamper. When there isn't space for a laundry container in the bedroom, see if you can make room in the closet.

OPPOSITE PAGE This headboard also serves as a nightstand and bookshelf.

TOP RIGHT Use hatboxes or baskets to store accessories or seasonal clothes when you don't have space in the closet.

BOTTOM RIGHT Bulky items such as suitcases can be hard to accommodate in closets. Instead, use them in the bedroom as storage or a low table.

LEFT This arrangement of fresh flowers, small boxes for loose change and receipts, and a tray for jewelry puts the top of the dresser to good use while keeping it uncluttered.

RIGHT A multipurpose hanging rod can hold jewelry, scarves, and other accessories.

BELOW Sort jewelry by color or style and use drawer dividers to keep all the small pieces organized.

INTERIOR DESIGNER
LORI DENNIS ON

Displaying Accessories

One way to utilize wall space between the bedroom and bathroom is to create a display of hanging accessories. I'll hang belts, purses, and jewelry on hooks along the wall. Over the hook, a 3-inch-deep shelf is perfect for sunglasses and belt buckles. You can really get creative and end up with something beautiful that solves a storage problem.

Jewelry and Accessories

Whether you have just a few favorite pieces or an extensive collection, you may choose to display necklaces and earrings out in the open or to tuck them away. Jewelry boxes that match the style of your bedroom furniture can be placed on a dresser or a small desk to keep your things easily accessible. If you don't need a jewelry box, consider putting a small tray on the nightstand so you have a place for earrings and bracelets when you retire for the night. Avoid dumping all of your jewelry in a bag; things will get tangled, and small pieces will be hard to find.

When you have a large collection and some pieces don't get much use, hang them in a frame on the wall, like art, so you can enjoy at least looking at them. Hats and scarves can also look great hung on a wall.

Reading Areas

If you have the space, add a comfortable chair and ottoman or a chaise to a corner of the room. Install a light on the wall behind the chair and place a 12-inch-diameter table or a small, lidded basket to one side. This may become your favorite place to unwind with a book or magazine at the end of the day. It may also get adopted as the place for bedtime stories with the children. If possible, keep televisions out of the bedroom so it can remain a place for quiet relaxation.

A cozy chair for curling up with a book or talking on the phone makes restful use of extra space in the bedroom.

Guest Rooms

Keeping the office area organized makes clearing out for guests much easier.

Bedrooms that aren't needed year-round for people living in the home can be put to good use even when there are no guests visiting. The trick is to make the space homey and welcoming for the occasional overnight visitor while also having it well set up for some other particular purpose.

Sleep Spaces

Depending on the guests you normally welcome, you must decide whether you'll be best served by a queen bed, two twins, a lone twin, a full-size bed, or a queen with a twin trundle underneath. There are also daybeds that accommodate twin mattresses, or futon frames that can be used as a seating area when not folded flat as a bed. Consider using the space under a guest bed for seasonal storage. A small dresser next to the bed can serve as a nightstand and as the place for your guests to put their things. Put a lamp on the dresser or install wall sconces over the bed for reading.

Work Spaces

Most often, families will use a guest room as the primary home office or as an extra work space. While you can spread your things out most days of the year, it's helpful to have a system in place for when guests do arrive.

One way to provide a lot of storage space in the room is to fill a wall with bookshelves interrupted by a cabinet with doors that can shut to hide the computer area when guests are staying with you. If a stand-alone desk makes more sense for your guest room, keep it small and look for one with a fold-down front that can be closed to hide the clutter. Use baskets or movable filing boxes for your personal papers so you can easily transport them to another room when necessary.

If you use the guest room as a place to exercise, try to corral your yoga mat, weights, and other gear in a basket or trunk at the end of the bed. Exercise DVDs can be stored without their cases in a small CD holder, along with your equipment. If you can, hang a flat-screen TV on the wall so it doesn't take up too much space in the room; use the computer or an iPod for your workout music. Large exercise equipment is harder to conceal when your houseguests arrive. Consider situating your stationary bike or elliptical machine in a corner of the room and have a folding-screen room divider that can at least partially hide the machine.

TOP In and out boxes under the small desk in this guest room can be removed and the desk can be shifted to the side when the futon couch needs to extend into a bed.

BOTTOM LEFT This twin bed is used as a window seat but can also be made up as a bed when there are overnight guests.

BOTTOM RIGHT When the closet in the guest room is otherwise occupied, install hooks on the wall for your visitors to hang clothes.

Nurseries

The opportunity to create a beautiful space for a new baby brings out the interior designer in most parents. While making it unique and adorable is the enjoyable part, making it safe and organized is not to be overlooked. Avoid bringing toxins into the nursery by using VOC-free paint on the walls, nontoxic finishes on floors and furniture, and solid-wood furniture rather than pieces made of particleboard. While babies can't get into too much trouble at first, in no time at all they're crawling, then walking. So it's a good idea to clear the nursery of anything they might topple—floor lamps, for example—or things they might get tangled in, such as window-shade cords.

Furniture

Nurseries don't need a lot of furniture early on, but ideally you will have a crib, a changing table, and a chair for feedings. Cribs are large for young babies, so you might start with a smaller-footprint bassinet. Or you may decide to buy a crib that will convert into a toddler bed when the child no longer needs to be contained at night. Buy a solid-wood dresser and attach a changing pad to the top instead of buying a separate changing table. This way you can continue using the dresser as the baby grows older. The top drawers can hold diapers and wipes, and you'll have fresh clothes right at hand. Lotions and baby powder can be kept on a

LEFT Wall-hung magazine racks allow you to display story-books almost as art in the nursery.

TOP RIGHT Square drawer dividers keep booties and baby gear organized.

BOTTOM RIGHT Colorful, labeled nesting containers store little things.

shallow shelf on a wall to the side of the dresser. Don't put anything right above the changing table or you'll risk having something fall on the baby.

Keeping Small Things Organized

Dresser drawers can easily become cluttered with tiny socks, diapers, and accessories. Keep them organized with standard drawer dividers sold for kitchens and bath-rooms. Small baskets and boxes can store little shoes and extra bedding.

LEFT A simple white bookshelf provides great storage and is timeless; you'll never have to replace it.

BELOW Meaningful items are stored together in a small box to be tucked away for safekeeping.

OPPOSITE PAGE An armoire is the ideal first closet for a baby. Use the center rod and open doors to hang and display special clothes. This example also includes a bag for laundry and swinging arms for blankets.

Displaying Keepsakes

There are so many firsts, meaningful events, and heartfelt gifts to cherish in a baby's life: the first pair of shoes, a vintage silver rattle, a sweater knitted by a friend. Use some of these things to decorate the nursery. Shallow shelves, open armoires, and hooks on the wall can all display small treasures. Interior designer Lori Dennis likes to use shadowbox frames in the nursery. "Display the first pair of shoes in a shadowbox frame, or a sampling of the shoes worn in the first year of life," Dennis suggests. "Or frame your favorite baby dress and hat and hang it on the wall."

Kids' Rooms

These pullout bins teach young children the alphabet and help them put their belongings away by themselves.

As children grow and accumulate clothes, toys, and hobbies, their rooms can become disaster areas. This doesn't have to be the case, however. If everything has a place, the child has no excuse for not keeping things organized.

Organizing Small Things

Many of the items in a child's room are small, so the containers should be sized accordingly. Take advantage of the bedroom door and the back of the closet door. These are great spots for over-the-door shoe holders—the small pouches will accommodate things such as shoes, hats, and toys.

If children can't see an item, they tend to forget about it. If your child has a large collection of toys, store some in the garage for a while, then bring them back into rotation. Keeping everything in large, deep toy chests will make things difficult to find, which means the contents are apt to wind up on the floor. By contrast, low shelves keep toys visible and accessible. Add bins and baskets to contain smaller items on the shelves. Avoid lidded containers, as kids tend not to open them and don't like having to put lids back on. Help children keep things organized by labeling baskets or using color-coded liners so they know the dolls go one place, the train set pieces another.

Buy tempered-glass or plastic containers for collections of small things that don't get much use, such as toy soldiers, marbles, or coins. Organized by color on a higher shelf, these items can become part of the room's decor.

TOP RIGHT Plastic or canvas shoe holders can be used to organize small toys.

BOTTOM RIGHT Canvas containers and baskets corral toys and books and can be moved from room to room.

Furniture

Cavernous bedroom closets are not particularly useful for small children's clothing. The space may be better utilized temporarily for your own storage. If there's space in the room, a freestanding cabinet with one hanging rod and narrow shelves for folded clothes and shoes will be more helpful for small items. Later, add more shelves where hanging clothes used to go, and the piece can be turned into closed storage for sweaters and school supplies.

Interior designer Lori Dennis likes to use basic white cabinets in kids' rooms. "Dress them up by pasting wallpaper on the back of each shelf," she suggests. "Then change the pattern as the child grows, and it completely updates the look of the room without buying new furniture."

In small rooms, floor space is hard to come by. When two children share a room, bunk beds make great use of the space, presuming a child is old enough to sleep safely on the top bunk. A trundle bed is a better option for very young children, since the lower bed is close to the ground and can be tucked away when not in use. For children who need desk space in the bedroom, consider a top bunk bed sold without the lower bunk. The area under the bed can be used for study. Another approach is to put a twin bed under the top bunk in an L-shape. This arrangement gives you two beds and desk space without taking up much additional floor space.

TOP LEFT These wall-hung shelves with a hanging rod are available in many styles and finishes, so you can coordinate them with other elements of the room. They're perfect for hanging small shirts and jackets.

TOP RIGHT Color-coded pails and cubbies help children learn where toys go.

BOTTOM Bunk beds keep floor space open for other activities.

OPPOSITE PAGE A floating desk keeps the room looking open and uncluttered and provides plenty of space for homework and art projects.

DESIGN CONSULTANT
KATE PARKER ON

Timeless Furniture

I prefer using adult furniture in kids' rooms. The important thing is to buy well-made pieces in classic styles. When the kids are young, paint the dresser a bright color. Down the line, you can repaint it or strip it to see the wood grain. This way you're not constantly buying new furniture as they grow.

Display

Children love to have an impact on their own space. Because their tastes evolve quickly, coming up with a method for accommodating changes will spare your walls and give kids the freedom to alter things themselves.

Instead of taping or pinning posters and art to the walls, hang a string horizontally across the top of one or more walls. Then hang shorter strands off the line so the kids can clip art or posters to them. You can make your own version of this system or buy one of the prepackaged products on the market.

Professional organizer Sara Eizen recommends these clip systems to her clients. "But that's just one way to save your walls," she advises. "You can also paint closet doors with magnetic paint, then cover it with the paint color of your choice, so kids can hang things with magnets." Another quick and easy idea is to cover acoustical ceiling tiles or cork tiles with fabric and hang them on the wall to form a bulletin board. "Combine several tiles together for a larger display. All of these ideas give kids the option to decorate their room as they please," Eizen says.

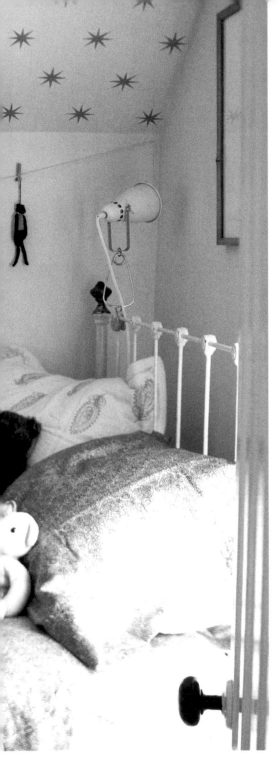

LEFT Toy monkeys hang from a string stretched across one wall. Next week, the child can use the same system to hang her newest favorite things.

TOP RIGHT Three rows of ribbon and wood clothespins display family photos in a Victorian-style child's room.

BOTTOM RIGHT Use vintage cards as a border around the edge of the room. These are framed with painted wood molding.

What do you do with older art when you need the space for new pieces? Professional organizer Sylvia Borchert suggests keeping a portfolio of all the pictures your kids bring home. At the end of the year, go through the box and edit the collection to the best or most meaningful drawings. Take a moment to write the child's name and the year on the backs of the pieces you're saving, then transfer them into an archival box to protect them from wear and tear.

Chapter 6

Closets

A good closet is a terrible thing to waste. If your closets don't stay organized, you're either trying to stash too many things in them or you don't have the right storage systems in place. Once you remove everything you don't need—all of those things you tossed in the closet because you didn't know what else to do with them—you're ready to come up with an effective system of hanging rods, shelves, and cubbies that will keep your belongings organized for the long haul.

When you have a well-
organized closet,
doors are optional.

No matter what type of closet you need to reorganize, the same basic principles apply. Block out some time in your schedule for a thorough inventory and cleanout. Get started by taking every last item out of the closet. No, you can't skip this part! Everything must come out, including the hangers. Move things to an adjoining room or any large, empty space.

Then start organizing your things by type. If it's a bedroom closet, put all the pants together, all the shoes together, all the suits together. If it's a utility closet, put all the tools together, all the cleaning supplies together. You get the idea.

Paring Down

The next step is to get rid of what you don't want or don't need—remember, the end result is supposed to be no clutter. The goal is not to have any more than you can fit. For some people, this is the hard part. Design consultant Kate Parker suggests starting by moving the things you definitely want to keep to a new pile. "It's a more positive approach than starting by forcing yourself to select what you're getting rid of," she explains. Once all of your no-brainers are in the "keep" pile, give some thought to the items that remain. For clothing, ask yourself if you would buy it today. If you don't remember the last time you wore a particular garment but you still don't want to get rid of it, resolve to start a clothing diary or come up with some other way to track what you're actually wearing over the course of a season (see pages 116–117).

Disposing of Unwanted Items

As you get to the bottom of the piles, start sorting what remains into separate boxes or bags for things you can give to friends and family, things you can donate to a local charity, and things you can sell online or at a garage sale. "If you have a favorite charity in mind, selecting things to get rid of can be a lot easier," Parker advises. "It feels so good to help a cause you care about that you might find you're letting go of more than you thought you could." Aim to throw away as little as possible and look for opportunities to recycle the items in your trash pile.

Closet Systems

Once you have sorted through your belongings, you're ready to consider a closet organizing system. Do not jump to this step until you've pared your belongings. Otherwise you might waste money on an elaborate system that you don't really need.

Start by drawing a sketch of the closet, marking the inside and door dimensions. Then measure the remaining clothes you need to hang, grouping long and short items separately. Fold and stack your sweaters and gather shoes, hats, ties, and accessories. Also fold and stack linens and towels for hall closets, and group cleaning supplies for utility closets. Measure each grouping so you can start to think about how many short rods, long rods, shelves, and drawers you'd like to have. Make a first pass at fitting everything onto your closet drawing.

Shopping for a System

Home improvement centers and organizing stores offer several brands of closet systems. Coated-wire systems are generally the least expensive, and they allow air movement around clothes. Mats are sold for shelves where small items would fall through the openings. Solid shelving systems are generally melamine—resin-coated particleboard—though you can find solid wood or engineered options made with low-VOC finishes and formaldehyde-free adhesives. These systems often hang on wall-mounted tracks; you can mix and match rods, shelves, and drawers. Most are easy to install, presuming you're relatively handy. Just make sure that you hit wall studs and that the tracks are level. The rest is pretty much foolproof. Built-in wood systems require some additional tools and skills.

Many stores have closet experts who can take your drawing and propose a system for your particular needs. "But they only know what you show them and don't usually come to the house," warns professional organizer Sylvia Borchert. "I think there's great value in having an organizer work through a closet with you, so they can help you utilize what you already own and customize a solution that works for you. For example, closet system software defaults to standard heights, resulting in rods that may be too high for you. An organizer can come up with a drawing that takes everything into consideration, and the closet system company can execute that plan."

Hall and Utility Closets

This hall closet was transformed into a craft space with rolls on the wall for wrapping paper and ribbon, clips and hooks for tissues and CDs. A shallow shelf holds tiny accessories. A worktable is mounted on the inside of the closet door—just flip it down, and it balances on the white leg.

H all closets are generally small, with a single hanging rod and a shelf. For most households, this doesn't quite solve all the problems. "You do not have to accept where the hanging rod is," advises professional organizer Sara Eizen. "For families with small children, get rid of the shelf and have one higher bar and one lower bar that kids can reach. This doubles the amount of hanging space." Only shoes that people wear most often should be in the hall closet. The rest should be kept in the bedrooms.

Maximizing Door Space

Over-the-door racks made for shoe storage can be useful in hall and utility closets for items other than shoes. Those little pockets can keep dog leashes, sunblock, gloves, and tools organized. If you store more hanging things in the closet, install hooks on the inside of the closet door for kids' jackets, purses, reusable grocery bags, scarves, and hats.

Going Vertical

When you use the closet to store mostly small or bulky items, remove the rod and go vertical. Install shelves outfitted with baskets or bins to keep things from migrating. Label the front of each container so you will know which one to grab when you're looking for something. It takes a lot less time to rifle through a small box than to search the entire utility closet for the grout cleaner or a crescent wrench.

Professional organizer Monica Ricci advises her clients not to set things like brooms and dust mops on the floor leaning against the wall. "Instead, hang them on a nail. Or, I like to use adhesive hooks that can hold relatively light items and come off drywall without a mark," Ricci says. Cleaning supplies should be grouped together, easy to grab and go. If you store any cleaning supplies or tools in the utility or hall closet, however, remember to childproof the door if there are young kids about.

ABOVE The left side of this closet includes shelves for household items. A lower rod makes jackets easy for children to grab.

LEFT Canvas and metal bins contain extra linens on open shelves.

BELOW Glass canisters hold bulk cleaning supplies. Label solid baskets so you know what's inside.

INTERIOR DESIGNER
LORI DENNIS ON

Pegboard

J ulia Child used pegboard to keep her pots and pans organized over the stovetop, and I like to use that same concept in utility closets. Outline what tool goes where so that everyone knows where to put things back. It's great for everything from hammers to flashlights to rolls of packing tape. If you ever move, your personalized pegboard can go with you.

Bedroom Closets

OPPOSITE PAGE This perfectly balanced his-and-hers closet does everything right. It includes a dresser and baskets for folded clothing and accessories, low drawers for shoes, clothes hanging airily on rods, and even high shelves for matching luggage.

TOP RIGHT An armoire with glass doors provides extra hanging and folded clothing storage in a bedroom.

BOTTOM RIGHT Pare down your clothing so you have room for new acquisitions.

People tend to wear about 20 percent of their clothes 80 percent of the time. So when you're sorting out which clothes to keep or discard (see pages 110–111), consider how often you actually wear things. If you aren't sure, start the new closet with all the hangers facing one direction. In the coming year, every time you wear a garment, put it back with the hanger facing the opposite way. At the end of each season, you will see clearly what you have never used. "You can do the same thing with folded clothing," suggests professional organizer Sara Eizen. "Start with everything inside out or oriented in a different direction."

Organize everything you've decided to keep either by use, by color, or by frequency of use. Design consultant Kate Parker loves the look of wood hangers, but they take up too much space in most closets. Instead, she suggests getting space-saving slim hangers covered with a velvety material so that clothes are less likely to fall off. "These will allow you to put so much more on each rod and give the closet a cohesive look," Parker says. Transfer all the remaining clothes to the new hangers, and you're ready to put everything back in the closet.

INTERIOR DESIGNER
KIT DAVEY ON

Shopping in Your Closet

Going through your old clothes may make you realize you have more than you thought you did. I encourage clients to go on a shopping spree in their own closets. Mix and match pieces you have never worn together before and take pictures of what you come up with so you remember what you own. You may save thousands of dollars a year this way.

Deep and Walk-In Closets

Closets that have at least 4 feet of space from the back wall can be useful for housing dressers and laundry baskets in addition to hanging clothes. Consider putting a low dresser with three to six drawers in the center of the wall. Hang long clothing on either side and shorter garments above it. You may even have a foot or two of clearance over the dresser so you can use the surface for hats or jewelry boxes. Use the 12 to 18 inches of sidewall space past the 2 feet of hanging clothing for vertical shelves or cubbies. Store shoes, accessories, and extra linens in this space.

If you have very deep or wide closets, there's great opportunity to make the space hardworking and functional. If the walk-in closet is visible from the bedroom or bathroom, consider having custom wooden built-ins made for the space, designed to look like an extension of the cabinetry in the rest of the house. This may be costly, but—just as in a kitchen remodel—it allows you to really take stock of your needs and devise the best ways to keep everything organized.

Shallow drawers can house ties, socks, and lingerie, sorted by style or color. Cabinets can be sized to accommodate suit jackets, blouses, or slacks behind separate doors. You can opt for glass doors so that clothes are visible but are kept dust-free. And you can light the space inside each cabinet so that every-thing is easy to see.

This is the no-expense-spared sce-nario. If you don't have the budget for such a solution, you can still make your walk-in closet into something special. Store-bought closet systems (see

ABOVE LEFT In a deep but narrow closet, a hanging rod is combined with drawers on wheels. Shoes are stored on top of the dressers, while the opposite wall contains hooks for robes, jackets, and accessories.

ABOVE RIGHT This walk-in closet with cubbies on one side and hanging rods on the other has pocket doors at each end, making it accessible from the bedroom or bathroom.

OPPOSITE PAGE, TOP Large walk-in closets can appear cluttered because of their sheer size, but this one looks organized and airy, thanks to solid mirrored doors on one side and muslin curtains on the other.

OPPOSITE PAGE, BOTTOM Custom built-in cabinets give a certain weight and permanence to walk-in closets that are not hidden from adjacent living spaces.

pages 112–113) are one solution. Or you can mix and match clothing rods, bookshelves, and armoires that may not have been made specifically for a closet. Dining room cabinets or armoires with solid or glass doors are great for sweaters and linens. Put one or more on a wall divided by hanging rods. You'll still get the benefit of separate shelves that will protect your clothes from dust, but without the custom price tag.

Throughout this book, you will see pictures of storage ideas in every room. Flip through it once more with your closet in mind to see how many solutions can be made to work for these storage spaces as well. By thinking creatively, you can repurpose everything from bookshelves to wooden crates and come up with a perfectly efficient closet.

Hanging Clothing

All of the experts on our design panel agree that although wood hangers look nice, it's better to use slim hangers so you can fit more on the rod. But whichever type of hanger you choose, start your new closet with all the same type. That way, everything will be at the same level and look uniform, and your eyes will spot things more easily. "I prefer to hang pants rather than use pant-clip hangers because it's easier," says interior designer Kit Davey. "If you have to take the hanger off the rod, lay it down, and use two hands to clamp the pants in place, you'll avoid taking that time to hang up your pants." Return any wire hangers to your dry cleaner for recycling.

Folded Clothing

It's better to have small cubbies, rather than long spans of shelves, for folded clothing. Sweaters stacked too high will fall over, and a row of folded clothing will soon meld together, tempting you to stuff clothes on the shelf rather than take the time to reorganize the piles. Cubbies that can contain two to three pieces of folded clothing are ideal. If you already have long shelves, get lined baskets to contain each stack. The lining will prevent the basket from snagging clothing. Lidded

plastic tubs won't let clothes breathe, but they will protect garments from bugs. If your closet is too small for folded clothing, look to the bedroom or other spaces in the house.

Seasonal and Special-Occasion Clothing

Try to store only what you're currently wearing in your bedroom closet. If possible, keep special-occasion garments and seasonal clothing in a guestroom or a hall closet. "Put seldom-used clothing that's worth keeping, such as tuxedos and holiday dresses, in cotton garment bags to keep the dust off," says professional organizer Monica Ricci. "Don't keep them in the plastic they came in long term."

Professional organizer Sylvia Borchert works on both coasts and points out that seasonal clothing can be a big issue in some places while not in others. "On the East Coast, you need gloves, hats, seasonal clothing, and outerware, and it all needs a place to go," Borchert says. "On the West Coast, there's less turnover." People who live in cold climates typically spend time each fall and spring boxing up last season's clothes to store in the garage or the attic and moving the next season's clothes into the closet. It's more work, but it gives you an opportunity to clean out the closet at least twice a year.

OPPOSITE PAGE, LEFT A hanging sweater organizer provides more space for folded clothes in a closet.

OPPOSITE PAGE, RIGHT Matching hangers give the closet a harmonious look and let your eye focus on the clothes.

RIGHT Hang a bold-patterned wallpaper in the guest closet and leave the doors open so it becomes part of the room's decor. Hooks can hold your special-occasion clothing or be left empty for guests.

Tied-back curtains instead of solid doors create a relaxed feel. Open baskets on the floor contain shoes.

Shoes

Shoes left uncontained on the closet floor, under hanging clothes, can easily get out of control and dusty. If you have nowhere else for the shoes to go, organize them by color or by season and store them in lidded boxes or baskets. Tiered racks, just like those used for plates in the kitchen, can also keep shoes organized. This is a good solution for daily-wear shoes that need to air out. Special-occasion shoes can be stored in the boxes they came in.

There are many designs for standing and hanging shoe racks, but most of them seem to take up more space than they should. Our design panel recommends using hanging or over-the-door shoe racks for anything but shoes—scarves, men's ties, accessories—because they simply don't hold many pairs. This is particularly true if you have clogs, boots, or heels.

Professional organizer Jen M. R. Doman prefers the canvas sweater bags that hang on a clothes rod for shoes. "Each pocket can hold three or four pairs of shoes, or even eight pairs of sandals. It's a more realistic solution for the number of shoes most people have," Doman says. Men's shoes are generally larger, so they will take up more space in the hanging canvas bags. Small wooden cubbies are another great way to keep shoes organized and visible.

Door Options

Closet doors that swing open into the bedroom can take up precious floor space. When you have a well-organized closet, there's no need to hide it. Consider removing the doors and replacing them with hanging curtains. It's a great way to add color and texture to the wall of a room rather than have a large span of closet doors.

Sliding doors don't impede on the bedroom, but they can be frustrating in that you can get into only one side at a time and you can't use the backs of the doors for storage. Consider replacing them with bifold doors that allow you at least to see the entire closet at once, or replace the doors with curtains.

Classic hinged doors offer space to hang hooks on both sides if you need additional storage space. Pottery Barn creative director Celia Tejada encourages people to decorate their closet doors. "The closet can be really sexy and personalized," Tejada says. "Use boldly printed wallpaper to line the inside of the closet doors to express yourself and make it fun."

ABOVE Resin-paneled doors with decorative reeds keep the closet bright but partially hidden from view.

RIGHT Photos taped to the end of each shoebox make finding the perfect pair of shoes much quicker and easier.

Kids' Closets

J ust as with keeping your children's rooms organized, planning their closets is an exercise in small. You'll have more success if you can size the solutions to the items actually being stored, which means little boxes, little bins, low and shallow shelves, and short hanging rods.

Many young children don't have much hanging clothing, and what they do have is short enough that it doesn't need the space allotted in an adult-size closet. Depending on the size of the bedroom, you may decide to use a freestanding armoire for a child's closet. That way you can use the built-in closet for your own things or turn it into toy storage. Or you can put in a dresser for folded clothes or cubbies for toys while keeping the hanging rod where it is for now. As the child gets older, add a second hanging rod lower down so she can reach her own things. The higher rod can be used for special-occasion or seasonal clothing.

LEFT Removing the closet doors makes it easier for kids to get their own clothes. Here, a store-bought rod system provides room to hang clothes at three levels.

TOP RIGHT Middle-school-aged children can put away their own clothes and shoes, if given a system that works for them.

BOTTOM LEFT Labeled sacks on shelves keep small clothes, shoes, and toys organized.

BOTTOM RIGHT Size the container for the items you need to store.

Closet doors can be used to hang small clothing on hooks, and over-the-door storage solutions sold for shoes are great for more folded kids' clothing and accessories. If you don't need the extra storage surface, professional organizer Jen M. R. Doman prefers removing the closet doors in kids' rooms. "When the door is too heavy or the knob is too high, children become more dependent on help," Doman explains. "Instead of a door, I'll install a tension rod or window-treatment pole across the closet opening and put up a shower curtain on metal rings. Metal on metal flies fast, so it doesn't take much strength to open it." Choose a plastic shower curtain that will stand up to greasy hands, or a natural fabric that can be tossed into the washing machine.

Teens' Closets

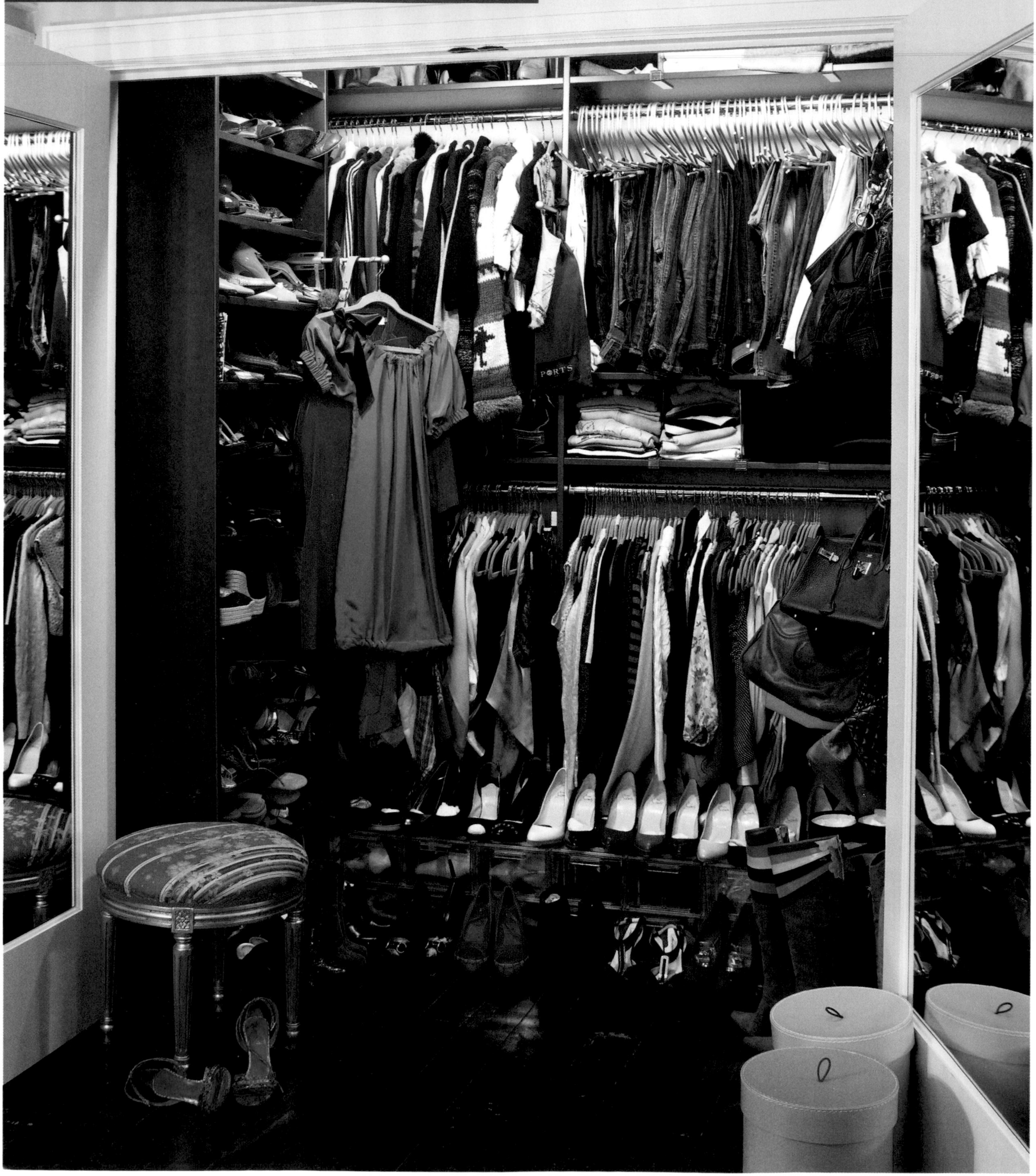

As children grow into teenagers, their closets will need a makeover. Suddenly they require more space for hanging clothes, a larger selection of shoes, room for special outfits such as sports uniforms or dancing clothes, and an array of accessories such as jewelry and purses. Because it might be the only space in the house a teen has for all of her belongings, the closet may also need to contain sports or art equipment, musical instruments, or childhood items she wants to save.

The overall goal should be to equip the space with enough hanging rods, shelves, baskets, and bins that she will never have a reason not to put something away. Teen closets are often overcrowded with clothes kids no longer like or may have outgrown. Make going through their closets a semiannual activity so they can pass things on to younger siblings, friends, or a local charity. Professional organizer Monica Ricci likes to put a laundry sorter in teen closets "both to encourage them to keep clothes off the floor and to teach them to sort and do their own laundry."

If you already have a low hanging rod in the closet, teens can use that for shirts and jackets. Add a higher rod for dresses, slacks, and special-occasion clothing. As with adult closets, a standing dresser or tower of wire baskets may be a great solution for folded clothing, shoes, and accessories.

OPPOSITE PAGE This walk-in closet is a teenage girl's paradise, with plenty of space for shoes, hanging clothing, and purses. Mirrors on both doors allow her to check the back as well as the front of an outfit.

LEFT Keep sports or dance-related clothing separate from school clothing.

ABOVE Wallpaper and creative displays give a teen's closet a little personality. These horizontal cubbies are divided by white watering cans.

Chapter 7

Work Spaces

No matter what you do for a living, chances are you need a place for occasional work at home. Spend some time coming up with a plan tailored to your precise needs—whether it's a small area for checking e-mail and paying bills or a fully equipped home office—and you can set yourself up with an efficient work space that requires little attention, other than the monthly filing of paperwork. This chapter has ideas for a variety of places that can accommodate a small work area, as well as proven ideas for keeping any office uncluttered and efficient.

Need more storage space in your office? Go vertical.

Home Offices

OPPOSITE PAGE
Family photos on the wall above the desk make the work space feel more like an extension of the home.

TOP RIGHT Spruce up an old desk by covering its surface with wallpaper and topping that with a piece of clear glass.

BOTTOM RIGHT You would never see eccentric knobs like these on a file cabinet in a corporate office.

More people than ever before work from home, thanks to technology that makes us virtually there with our colleagues down the street or around the world. To preserve a healthy balance between your work and home life, however, it's beneficial to have a separate room for the home office. This can also sometimes win you a deduction on your taxes. Take advantage of the fact that you're working at home by not setting up an office that looks like your old cubicle. Instead of standard office furniture, buy a desk and filing cabinets that go with the style of the other furniture in your house.

"Bring your own personality into the space. Add some artwork and a comfortable chair for reading when you are not on the computer," advises interior designer Kit Davey. "This is your home, so you can express who you are. When you avert your gaze from the computer, it should land on something beautiful." Making the space feel like an extension of your home will leave most people happier and more productive. Keep this in mind when selecting flooring, paint colors, fixtures, and accessories.

Paring Down

Thanks to computers, the ease of sharing digital files, and managing accounts and payments online, many of us have less paperwork to store than we used to. Chances are, however, that you still have some old paperwork in your office that doesn't need to be there. Design consultant Kate Parker suggests looking up how long you need to save specific types of financial records, then culling out every-

thing you no longer need. "Schedule 15 minutes a day to shred these papers. Otherwise they'll continue taking up space in your office," Parker says.

In addition to removing old files, take some time to unsnarl the wires under your desk. Turn everything off, get rid of the tangles, bundle each wire so that it's only as long as it needs to be to reach its source, then plug everything back in. Tape or twist-tie the wires so they don't become spaghetti again.

Desk Area

Standard desks are approximately 30 inches high. This height works well for sorting papers or jotting a note, but if you will be typing on the computer for hours each day, the keyboard should be positioned just above your lap, so that your elbows are parallel to the floor while you're typing. Outfit a wooden desk with a low, retractable keyboard tray that you can pull out when you need it. Even if you typically use a laptop, equipping it with such an alternative keyboard will be kinder to your wrists. Consider hiring an ergonomics expert to analyze your workstation.

Everything Within Reach

"Consider the desk to be a sacred place and only have what you are currently working on covering the surface," advises professional organizer Sylvia Borchert. Avoid putting decorative objects on the desk. Everything you typically need should be within reach of your chair. Put in and out boxes on a shelf just above your desk. The files you access regularly can be on a rolling cart that's visible and at your fingertips.

Using the Closet

When you have turned a bedroom into a dedicated home office, you may be reluctant to include the closet, particularly if it's already in use storing clothes or other household items. But professional organizer Monica Ricci encourages clients to make the closet an integral part of the office. "It's a great way to keep the floor space free of clutter," Ricci says. "Take the clothes rods out and outfit the entire closet with shelves. Put all your reference books, filing boxes, and even electronic equipment, such as printers and shredders, into the closet. Close the door and everything is hidden away, plus books stay dust-free."

TOP There are baskets below and a variety of boxes and bins above, but the work surface stays clear.

BOTTOM LEFT A hanging wire basket maximizes storage space in the hutch above a desk.

BOTTOM RIGHT Raising the monitor to eye level keeps your head and neck straight. This platform also expands the surface area of the desk.

OPPOSITE PAGE A rolling cart under the desk and shelves above keep everything close at hand.

LEFT This rolling basket from Pottery Barn has a divider in the middle to help keep papers organized.

BELOW A stand-up rack is perfect for the files you need to access every day.

OPPOSITE PAGE, LEFT Magazines and narrow books are easier to find on an office shelf when kept in magazine holders. Note the contents on the spine of each box.

OPPOSITE PAGE RIGHT Three bins under the desk separate recycling, trash, and paper to be shredded.

Filing Solutions

It's so easy to get behind on office filing. Some days it feels as though just paying the bills and clearing off your desk are a major accomplishment, even if it means you threw everything into the "to be filed" stack in your office. Once a week or once a month, take your papers out to the living room. While you're watching something on television that doesn't require full attention, organize the papers and put them into their proper filing locations. If you let this task slide for months, it will only take longer when you get to it.

Come up with a filing system that is simple and makes sense for your situation. There are filing cabinets, baskets, and plastic tubs that can stow the files you need to keep for reference. These may not need to be visible in the office if you won't be consulting them regularly. If you run your own business, your filing system should mirror the categories you need to track for tax purposes. These are typically divided into subcategories for income and expenses.

Keep business and family files separate. Interior designer Kit Davey suggests making a list of all the files in each box and drawer with notes on what's stored where. This will leave you with a master list you can consult when you're looking for something specific. It will also eliminate the need to hunt through every box in the office, closets, and garage. Professional organizer Deborah Silberberg advises her clients to set up their paper files to match the organizational system they use on the computer. "Now that everything is a combination of paper and e-filing, those categories should correlate so you don't have to memorize two systems."

Baskets and Bins

Put three small baskets either under or beside your desk: one for trash, one for paper recycling, and one for shredding. If the recycling is kept this convenient, you'll have no excuse not to use it as you are filing or opening the mail.

Small bins and ceramic pots are useful on top of the desk to contain pens or paper clips. If you're working on several different projects at once, get a lidded basket, plastic tub, or metal bin for each one and keep the paperwork and accessories separate. Cardboard boxes should be used only for long-term storage in the garage. Everyday use causes them to deteriorate quickly.

PROFESSIONAL ORGANIZER
SARA EIZEN ON

Electronic Billing

One of the best ways to reduce the amount of paper you need to file is to sign up for electronic billing. If my clients don't already do this, we sit down together and sign them up on the spot. Then we enter the due dates into the calendar so nothing is forgotten about. This change eliminates clutter instantly.

POTTERY BARN
CREATIVE DIRECTOR
CELIA TEJADA ON

The Daily System

Our Daily System maximizes wall space in a creative way that's completely customizable. Wall-mounted stainless steel rods allow you to mix and match the number of accessories you want. Choose from dry-erase boards, cork boards, letter bins, or even digital frames. This system keeps your life visible but contained and off the work surface, and it solves organization problems for everyone from busy professionals to large families.

Shelves

Use bookshelves in the office for filing boxes and for holding baskets and books you use regularly. If you have space to keep lots of books in the office, put the reference books at eye level and the more sentimental or rarely used things at the top, such as old yearbooks and photo albums. Keep bookshelves airy (see pages 74–77) by interspersing picture frames or vases between stacks of books.

A few short and narrow shelves on the wall behind your desk can be used for in and out trays and for magazines or books that you need nearby. Keep magazines and slender publications in stand-up magazine holders and label them by subject or year. Label trays by subject or by the level of urgency, then take papers directly from your work bag and put them in the right ones. This will help ensure that things don't get lost or forgotten.

Drawers

Avoid turning office drawers into catch-all collectors by using drawer dividers or small boxes. Keep pens and pencils, calculators, clips and rubber bands, and paper separated so you can find what you are looking for quickly. Drawers should not be used for long-term storage. If you have things in drawers that you don't need access to on a regular basis, transfer them to filing boxes in the closet or garage.

Bulletin Boards and Calendars

There are many styles of bulletin boards available today, from simple corkboards to ones that are padded and covered with fabric and ribbon. Find something that matches the style of your office, or make one of your own using fabric that coordinates with your window treatments or chair. Use the bulletin boards for reminder notes, family photos, invitations, coupons, and gift certificates.

Many people use digital calendars these days, but it's also helpful to have a larger version of the current month on the wall so you can see at a glance what's coming next. A dry-erase board is a reusable solution, or you can hang an attractive calendar on the wall or prop up a weekly calendar on a shelf above your desk.

OPPOSITE PAGE, LEFT A few floating shelves and a CD holder keep essential items close at hand while preventing clutter on a small desk.

OPPOSITE PAGE, RIGHT Drawers around the desk area should be used for ready access rather than long-term storage.

ABOVE Cover a standard bulletin board with fabric to add color and texture to your office wall.

Alternative Work Areas

The trick to incorporating a work space into a living room is to keep the furniture and finishes cohesive in their appearance.

Not every home has a room to spare for use as the office, but we all need places to pay bills, run the household, check e-mail, or do homework. From laptops and moveable trays to unobtrusive desks, there are many ways to make efficient work possible in rooms normally used for other activities.

In a Bedroom

Keep bedroom work spaces small and uncluttered, particularly if they are in the master bedroom. Select a desk that goes with the rest of the furniture. If you use the desk only occasionally, opt for an upholstered chair rather than an ergonomically correct piece of office furniture. Interior designer Lori Dennis suggests putting a skirt on the front of the desk that coordinates with other fabrics in the room. "This hides the computer wires and makes it look more like a residential space," Dennis explains. Instead of a utilitarian desk lamp, use a bedside table lamp that matches others in the room. After each work session, put everything away in portable boxes or baskets hidden beneath the desk so that the restful ambiance of your bedroom is preserved.

Guest bedrooms are ideal for office spaces (see pages 96–97). Because these are not private spaces, however, you may need a system for securing your personal papers in movable boxes or locking file cabinets. If the guest-bedroom closet has sliding doors, put a divider between the two sides. Outfit one side of the closet with a hanging rod and dresser for your guests, or for your own seasonal clothing storage. The other side can be equipped with adjustable shelves for file boxes, books, and electronics.

To preserve space for the guest bed, exercise equipment, or whatever else you need in the room, confine your work space to a single wall. Lori Dennis suggests improvising a work surface with a piece of finished wood mounted along one wall, corkboard above it, and a few filing boxes below. "This uses the linear space in a room and keeps everything along one wall so that almost no floor space is used," she explains.

In the Living Room

A small desk in the living room allows you to work while keeping an eye on the kids or simply staying in proximity to other members of the household. A delicate desk behind the sofa or to the side of the room can blend in with its surroundings, or you may need something larger. The trick is to keep the desk surface from becoming a place where mail, papers, keys, and bike helmets accumulate. The best way to eliminate such problems is to set up organizing solutions for each of the items that might otherwise wind up on the desk.

TOP RIGHT White cubbies on wheels visually separate the living room and work space. Colorful storage boxes and magazine holders add to the style of the room.

BOTTOM LEFT Placed perpendicular to a built-in wall unit, this work area enjoys views of the backyard.

BOTTOM RIGHT A small dressing table with drawers in the corner of a bedroom doubles as a place for paying bills or catching up on correspondence.

DESIGN CONSULTANT
KATE PARKER ON

The Anywhere Office

Put together an office on a tray and you can work literally anywhere in the house. The tray contains stationery, pens, and a few envelopes and stamps. That plus a laptop and a wireless Internet connection is really all you need to get some work done.

In the Kitchen

In families with young children, the kitchen table may be in nearly constant use throughout the day—between their meals, art projects, and homework. Parents also may claim a corner of the table for paying bills and getting their own work done. If this becomes your go-to work space, keep a few baskets with lids or decorative boxes against the wall to store work materials. Kids should each have their own basket or cubby in which to keep their schoolwork.

If you're planning a kitchen remodel and you have the extra space, add a section of built-in cabinetry with drawers and a work surface to serve as a mini home office. An appliance garage can hide the computer and office accessories. Drawers can be outfitted as filing cabinets.

In the Dining Room

Just like the kitchen table, the dining room table is a wonderful place to spread out a project and get some work done. If you don't use the dining room table regularly, it can be an even better spot than the kitchen table because you don't have to clear it before most meals. Use space on the bookshelves or dining room buffet to store boxes of business paperwork or school supplies.

Under the Stairs

Don't let this prime real estate go unused. The angle of most staircases will accommodate a desk and a couple of wall-hung shelves. A small stool can be pushed under the desk when not in use, so it doesn't take up space in a narrow hallway. Or hire a finish carpenter to build cabinets and a work surface, equipping the unit with doors that can be closed to hide the area completely.

ABOVE LEFT A round breakfast table tucks into the side of built-in cabinetry that includes a small work area.

ABOVE RIGHT Across from the kitchen table, a built-in desk is a great place for kids to do homework while dinner is being prepared.

OPPOSITE PAGE A generously sized desk fits under the widest point under the stairs, while shelves follow the angle up the wall.

Small-Space Work Areas

Use a low shelf of a wall unit as a small workstation. Here, desk lamps attached to the face of the built-in illuminate the area.

You may not need or have space for a full desk setup. Work spaces can be squeezed into many areas of the house when you use small desks, low shelves of a wall unit, or wall-mounted desks that fold down as needed.

Design consultant Kate Parker points out that a laptop and a comfortable chair will allow you to make just about any area a work space. A padded tray to keep the warm laptop off your legs will even suffice for working on the couch. Store the tray under the couch or beneath a coffee table.

Look around your house and think creatively about where you might be able to squeeze in a work space. A landing area between flights of stairs, an upstairs hallway between bedroom doors, or a wall space between the living room and kitchen can all be suitable spots for a small desk. You'll need to keep the surface clear or at least organized, because it's out in the open, but you may prefer it to working on your lap in the living room.

TOP A wall of clipboards hanging over a small table makes this a multifunctional work space.

BOTTOM LEFT A wooden tray with a notebook and pens, a laptop, and a chair are really all you need.

BOTTOM RIGHT In a hallway, a floating cabinet holds work files, and the top can be used as a writing surface.

Hiding Work Areas

Armoires equipped with shelves and drawers can be used as small work-stations anywhere in the house. Open the doors and pull up a chair from the kitchen or dining room to work at the computer. There's space for your most frequently referenced files, but long-term storage should be kept elsewhere. The inside surfaces of the doors can be used to pin notes and calendars on cork board. When your work is done, simply close the doors and move the chair to the side so that your workstation is hidden from view.

Secretaries are small desks with fold-down fronts. Popular in the late 1800s and early 1900s, they can be found in antique stores; more newly minted versions are also available. Secretary desks are usually about 3 feet wide, and some have shelves or drawers under the fold-down desk surface. Inside there may be slots for mail and one or two small drawers. Such pieces of furniture are a great option for bedrooms, where you want a quiet area for occasional work but don't want to have to look at the bills or a messy desk when you're trying to relax. As long as you don't put too much in a secretary, you should be able to close it each night.

TOP LEFT Secretary desks, like this one from Pottery Barn, are discreet and ideal for small spaces.

BOTTOM LEFT This Pottery Barn cabinet with a hutch and a fold-down work area is perfect for storage and display in a hallway.

RIGHT Setting up an office inside a closet gives you plenty of storage space. With the door closed, you'd never know the work space was there.

Chapter 8

Entries and Mudrooms

Stop clutter at the source by assigning a set place for everything you carry through the front door on a daily basis. Depending on the number of people living in your home and the nature of their activities, you may find that a simple bench and a few baskets will do. Other households may need more elaborate cabinet and cubby systems to stay organized. Whichever solution meets your needs, the goal is to have a plan for the things that might otherwise clutter the house as you enter and an easy way to reassemble your gear quickly as you leave.

A hardworking entryway needn't look the part.

Entryways

An organized entryway with a bench, cabinets, drawers, and cubbies ensures that nothing you bring in has to find a home for itself much beyond the front door.

The area just inside the front door can easily become a jumble unless you have a system to prevent the clutter. If there's nowhere handy to hang your coat, it will probably wind up draped over a chair—or on the floor if a child is involved. Shoes, mail, work bags, gym bags, backpacks, the dog's leash—there's actually quite a range of things you need to set down as you walk in the door throughout the day. Setting up a system for where everything goes will ensure that the mess doesn't migrate too far into the house.

Consoles

Even if your entry is a narrow hallway, there's generally at least enough wall space available for a low, shallow console table. A table that is open underneath or one with a single drawer will keep small entryways from looking crowded. You will get more out of the area, however, if there's a cabinet or shelves under the table for storing bags and shoes. Or you can place a few baskets under the table to accommodate those items. Design consultant Kate Parker has a mini vintage dresser the size of a nightstand near her front door. "There's a little drawer where I throw keys and mail, and I try to keep the top clear except for a pretty vase and a picture. For one or two people, this may be all you need," Parker says.

Shelves

Simple shelves, either by themselves or used in conjunction with hooks, give you a place to set mail and keys. One or more floating shelves matched to the trimwork in the rest of the room will be visually cohesive. Add a couple of shallow in and out boxes to separate what came in with you from what you need to take with you as you leave. A small basket on the shelf for keys and cell phones will help you remember to grab those items as you dash out the door.

TOP LEFT In a narrow hallway, a console table with a lower shelf takes up little room and it helps keep the rest of the house uncluttered.

TOP RIGHT Hang a key holder next to the front door so you don't lose time searching for your keys each morning. This holder has a mail slot as well.

BOTTOM A floating shelf between two half walls allows for plenty of storage space underneath.

LEFT This narrow, vintage bench offers a place to sit and take off your shoes, which can be stored underneath.

OPPOSITE PAGE, LEFT This bench and shelf combination from Pottery Barn makes up for the lack of an entry closet. Both pieces have cubbies to stow daily use items, and hooks under the shelf keep coats and bags ready to go.

OPPOSITE PAGE, RIGHT Low hooks over a bench give kids a place to hang their coats.

Hooks and Coat Racks

No room for a console table? Install one hook per person in the household, plus two or three extras, along the wall to receive coats and purses. You can hang a lot in a small space by starting low on the wall. Kids get the hooks closest to the floor, while seldom-used hats and scarves can go toward the top of the wall. A circular coat rack is another option; on some models umbrellas can fit in the middle. Coat racks are also useful for stowing bags and leashes.

Shoes

The benefits of removing your shoes at the front door are significant and multifaceted. Shoes can carry into your home traces of any toxins or debris you may have walked through outside. If shoes are removed at the door, those particles won't end up in the dust accumulating on the floor, ready to be inhaled. The other difficulty with tracked-in toxins is that you can pick them up on your feet as you walk around the house, then carry them into your bed. With a no-shoe policy inside the house, people with wood or tile floors will only need to vacuum on a regular basis, rather than mop, to keep the floors clean.

Put a basket or two at the front door for people to deposit their shoes. Having a place to sit down is also helpful. Interior designer Lori Dennis suggests offering slippers to guests who don't want to go barefoot. "It's a nice touch, especially when visitors don't already know they'll need to remove their shoes and aren't prepared," Dennis says.

Multipurpose Storage Solutions

In narrow hallways or in homes where the front door opens right into the living room, there's little space for a dedicated entryway. Professional organizer Sylvia Borchert suggests looking for multipurpose furniture that blends with the rest of the room to solve common entryway dilemmas. "Go through a store or catalog and look for pieces that have the shape and purpose you're looking for. Choose storage solutions by purpose, not room. You may find the perfect thing for the entryway in the kitchen department, for example," Borchert says. Consider transplanting pieces that may have been intended for some other part of the house. If there's a lidded basket you like as the laundry hamper, for instance, think about having a second one by the front door to catch incoming backpacks.

Baskets and Buckets

A few baskets at the front door are all the organization some households need. Use one for shoes, one for mail, and a third for bags. Or use them in conjunction with hooks on the wall or under a small bench. Families with young children can use different colored basket liners to indicate whose basket is whose—part of teaching kids to put their belongings away. If possible, keep one empty basket near the front door for things that will need to be carried upstairs or to some other part of the house. Make it a sturdy basket with handles so you can use it to cart items to their proper destinations.

During winter, or if you live in a wet climate, it's wise to have a metal or plastic bucket near the front door for dripping umbrellas. It can be useful to keep a pan with sides against one wall to collect wet shoes; position a hook above the pan so jackets have a place to drip-dry.

Cubbies

Similar in concept to school lockers, although lacking the doors, cubbies provide personal space for members of the household. Assign a cubby to each person and include a hook or two, a narrow shelf, and a basket on the bottom. Each of these tall, narrow spaces can accommodate hats, bags, jackets, and shoes. They will keep everyone's belongings sorted out, and you can see immediately if something is missing.

Cabinets

Floor-to-ceiling cabinets that match the other woodwork in the house make for a seamless entryway, particularly if everything can be hidden behind closed doors. Plan for a built-in entry cabinet as you would for custom kitchen cupboards. Think about all the things you bring in and take out of the house on a regular basis. Measure items and make sure the cabinet will accommodate your favorite bags, sports equipment, and the bulkiest outerware. Design pullout shelves in bottom cabinets and assign lower storage spaces to the kids. Use higher shelves for seasonal items, such as hats and mittens, that aren't in everyday use.

If you'd like the look and functionality of a built-in cabinet but can't afford to make the investment right now, buy a wooden bookshelf and install crown molding around the top. Then outfit the shelves with baskets so that your belongings will be out of view. You'll get a similar look and comparable functionality.

ABOVE Built-in cabinets make the most of the space you have. These built-ins also function as a room divider, with frosted glass panels between the cabinets and ceiling.

TOP RIGHT A lined basket near the front entrance is useful for items that people drop off as they enter the house.

BOTTOM RIGHT These cubbies were custom made to hold four old mailboxes and four baskets—one for each member of the family.

Back Doors

Built-in cabinets adjacent to the back door match those in the kitchen nearby, making a small space highly functional.

The back entry is generally only for family members and friends, so the setup can be more utilitarian. In some houses, this might be the logical place for stowing coats and shoes, presuming it's an entrance that you commonly use. If this is the case, follow the suggestions for entryways on the previous pages. For people who more often use the front door but come through the back after gardening or using the swimming pool, assign places for your garden gloves and muddy shoes or keep a bucket to catch the towels wet from the pool. If the back door leads to a garage, designate a place for reusable shopping bags where you'll see them on your way out. This can also be a good place for a paper recycling bin, if it's on the usual path to the trash bins.

Interior designer Kit Davey likes the space around the back door as a main exit point. In addition to places for coats and bags, she suggests displaying the family calendar there. "If it's the one place in your house that everyone will walk through, it's the best spot for notes and for parents and kids to see what's on the agenda that day."

ABOVE LEFT Back doors are often the entry and exit point for pets as well as people. This setup includes a bed for the dog, plus cubbies for garden boots.

ABOVE RIGHT Repurposed lockers and a low metal coat rack set a suitably casual tone for this rear entrance.

RIGHT In a narrow hallway leading to the back door, shoes perch on a wooden box. There's also a row of hooks for coats, hats, and bags.

Mudrooms

Utilitarian aluminum shelves are perfect for keeping garden supplies organized.

Mudrooms are enclosed spaces typically off the back door, but they can also hang off a front door. While they used to be commonplace to keep harsh weather out of the main house, they have become more of a rarity. If you're lucky enough to have one, use it to its full storage and organizing potential by following the recommendations on the previous pages. Because the room is separate from the main house, you won't have to worry much about making the shelves or furniture match what's inside. Sometimes the mudroom can even accommodate sports and garden equipment, or the washer and dryer.

Sports Areas

Active families can use large mudrooms to store bikes, skateboards, and sports equipment—hockey sticks, skis, and the like. If you have the wall space, install hooks or brackets for such items so they are not underfoot. Hooks will also keep helmets and pads visible so you won't forget them on your way out the door.

Potting Areas

Gardening enthusiasts often create potting areas in their mudrooms. Use one wall for all the usual things you need to keep organized while entering and exiting the house. Another wall can be the garden center, with slatted shelves for pots and garden tools and a sink for soaking plants and washing up. Put a few hooks on the wall over the sink for towels and wet gloves.

Laundry Areas

Dual-purpose mudroom and laundry rooms attempt to fit a lot into a small space. But in many homes the mudroom is the ideal place for washers and dryers, as it keeps the noise away from the living areas. A stackable washer and dryer will allow you to fill the rest of the wall with floor-to-ceiling cabinets, cubbies, or shelves. Allocate some space for laundry detergent and other cleaning agents among your jackets and sports equipment. See chapter 9 for more on laundry rooms.

TOP RIGHT Mudroom shelves can also hold games and toys. Underneath, letter hooks remind kids which space is theirs.

BOTTOM RIGHT A wire organizing system works just as well in a mudroom as it does in a closet.

Laundry and Craft Rooms

Laundry rooms can be treated much like kitchens—select the right number of shelves and drawers to keep all the small things organized, then prevent clutter by making sure everything has a place to go. Craft areas are like closets and home offices in that they tend to involve numerous tools and materials, all of which need to be kept sorted and accessible. Look back through previous chapters with your laundry or craft space in mind, then check out the following pages for additional ideas.

This multipurpose cabinet and shelving unit includes locks on the lower doors to keep children away from cleaning products.

Laundry Rooms

A pullout wire basket in this built-in cabinet holds dirty clothes awaiting their turn in the washing machine.

In many households, the washer and dryer are situated in a hallway closet, in the garage, or next to the kitchen or a bathroom. In others, there is a dedicated room for these machines, usually with additional space for other household storage. If you have the opportunity to design a new laundry room, try to keep it close to where laundry originates—generally, near the bedrooms. This will allow you to avoid lugging dirty laundry up and down the stairs or back and forth from the garage.

In dedicated laundry rooms, there is no need to hide the machines with cabinetry. But it is helpful to have a good amount of counter space for folding and sorting laundry, and a sink for rinsing stains out of clothing. There will likely be room for a row of upper cabinets or shelves for storing detergent and mending kits. In most cases, there isn't all that much to store that relates specifically to the laundry, so you may have some extra space to hold emergency supplies or household cleaners above or beside the machines.

Sharing Space

Front-loading washers and dryers are more energy efficient than top-loading models, and they are also more flexible in where you can put them. In a kitchen, you can hide these appliances in a row of lower cabinets, as most models will fit under the standard countertop height. Alternatively, you can stack front-loading machines and put them in a floor-to-ceiling cabinet in a kitchen or bathroom. When the machines are close to main living spaces, noise can be an issue. Consider applying soundproofing foam inside the cabinets that house the machines to make them a bit quieter. Avoid louvered doors for the same reason. A bathroom ventilation fan in a closed closet will provide the necessary air exchange.

ABOVE LEFT Sliding wooden doors hide the machines in a kitchen. The slats allow for proper airflow but won't muffle the noise.

ABOVE RIGHT Simple wooden shelves in a laundry room give you plenty of space to store cleaning supplies and ironing tools.

Canvas baskets on
exposed shelves
hide the clutter.

Shelves and Caddies

There are storage devices made to fit the narrow gap between the washer and dryer, or between one of the machines and the wall or a cabinet. These narrow caddies roll out and keep laundry detergent and stain sticks close at hand. You can also install shallow shelves on the wall next to the machines and set your cleaning supplies there. Try not to use the tops of the appliances for storage of cleaning supplies. When your machines are both on the floor, that space can be used for sorting and folding, or for drying delicates on a rack. When the machines are stacked, the dryer will be on top and the vibrations may knock off whatever you put up there.

Hooks

A few rows of hooks along the wall inside the laundry area can make the most of a narrow space. Professional organizer Sylvia Borchert suggests laminating stain-removal tips from your favorite magazines and hanging them on a chain so you can quickly remind yourself how to handle everything from grass stains to splashes of red wine.

Hang a small bag for the lint from your dryer. "Gather all of your lint this way, and then throw it in with your compost at the end of each week, or sprinkle it throughout the garden," suggests interior designer Lori Dennis. The lint is biodegradable, however, only if it's from clothing made of natural fibers, such as cotton, wool, and linen.

ABOVE Recessed shelves require no space in the room and keep cleaning and ironing supplies within reach.

LEFT Keep a few small containers nearby for things found in pockets or for buttons that fall off.

Line-Drying Clothes

For savings on energy and to protect certain types of clothing, you may find that you wind up line-drying more items each week than you dry in the machine. However, line-drying large amounts of clothing requires quite a bit of space. In a laundry room, there are probably places where you can hang a closet rod for this purpose—or even several rods. One great place for a rod is between a run of upper cabinets and over a sink that will catch the drips. You can also hang clothes from a rod over the machines or from a clothesline spanning the room.

There are freestanding drying racks that can fit between the two machines, so you don't have to find floor space elsewhere. "Sometimes you can squeeze these in about two-thirds of the way open," says professional organizer Deborah Silberberg. "Not everything has to have the footprint it was made to fill. This can be a great way of using that small space for something worthwhile." When you need to find space for drying clothes in a bedroom or an office, look for racks that fold down from the wall or from the back of a door so they are out of the way when not in use.

Ironing Boards

It's a hassle to lug the ironing board from the closet to the bedroom or wherever you have room to perform this chore, but leaving it out all the time takes up valuable floor space. Instead, look for a spot where you can hang the ironing board inside a cabinet or on the back of a bedroom or office door. The downside to this solution is that it fixes in place your ironing station—sometimes in a cramped or confined space—which may not be suitable if you tend to iron large batches at once. It's perhaps a better idea for people who just need to do occasional touch-up ironing. If you do install a fixed ironing board, be sure to situate it in a position that allows you to iron with your preferred hand.

PROFESSIONAL ORGANIZER
MONICA RICCI ON

Wrinkle-Free Clothing

I keep a stack of hangers in the laundry room so that when clothes come out of the dryer I can hang them right away to keep them from wrinkling. If you don't have room to store hangers there, just toss one into the laundry hamper each time you put on a shirt that needs to be ironed. That way it will be waiting for you in the hamper after each load.

OPPOSITE PAGE, TOP LEFT A couple of handled buckets in the laundry area are useful for carting wet clothes to another room to dry.

OPPOSITE PAGE, TOP RIGHT Keep a jar of clothespins in each location where you line-dry clothing.

OPPOSITE PAGE, BOTTOM Consider installing a pop-up ironing board in a modified drawer in the laundry room or kitchen.

RIGHT A wire closet organizing system works beautifully in a laundry room for air-drying clothing.

Craft Spaces

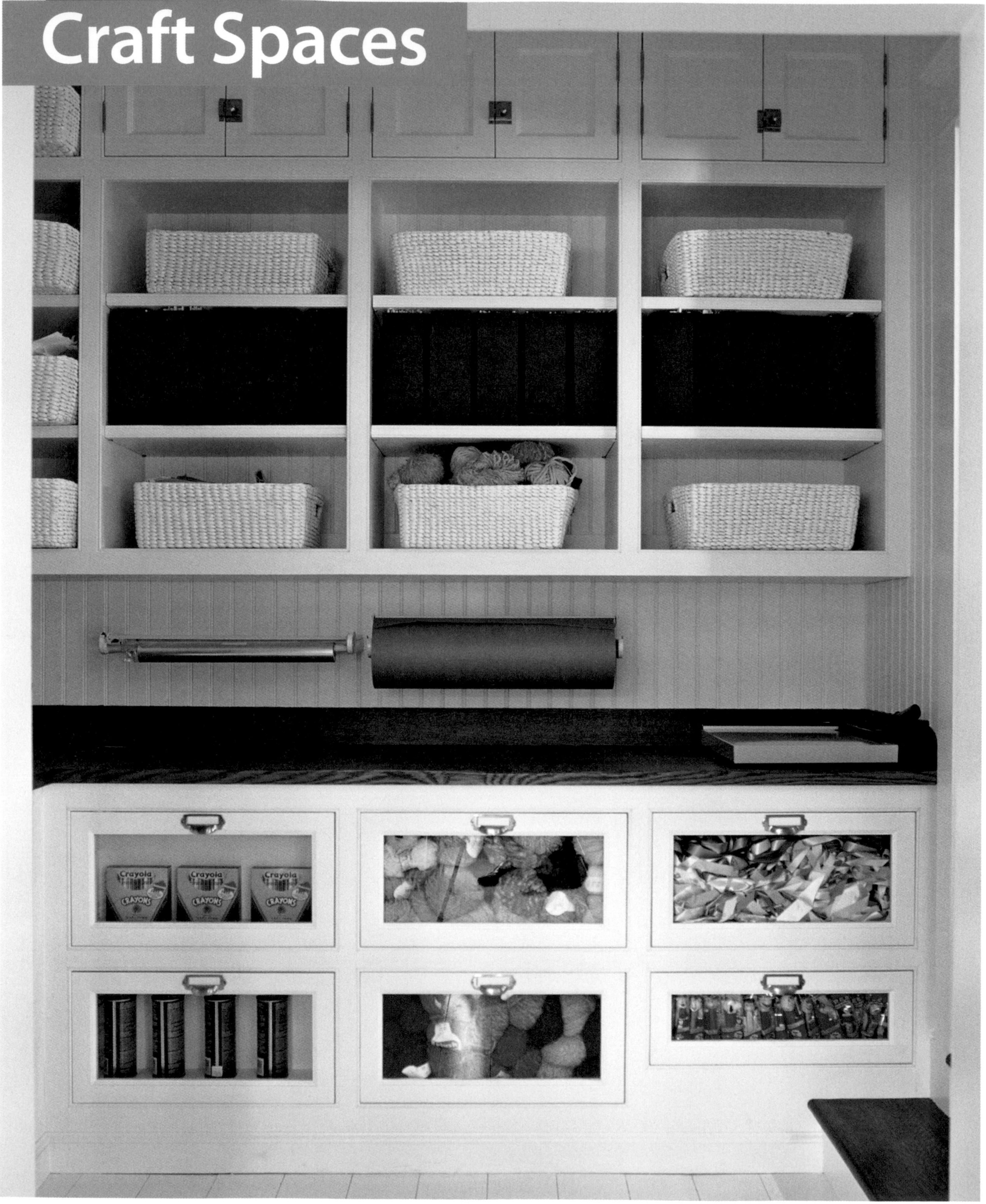

Just like kitchens, bathrooms, and kids' rooms, craft areas have lots of small items to be kept organized. The storage solutions that worked in those rooms may be equally well suited for your craft supplies. Pullout shelves, baskets, bins, hooks, and drawer dividers can all be used, even if they are marketed for some other purpose. Design consultant Kate Parker encourages clients to use kitchen and home-office storage solutions for craft spaces. "For example, spice racks are perfect for storing and sorting things like glitter and buttons," she says. "And magazine racks keep specialty papers organized." In similar fashion, stand-alone paper-towel racks work well for spools of ribbon.

Whether you do your crafts in a guest room, in a laundry room, or on the kitchen table, make sure you have plenty of countertop space and adequate lighting. In a closet or on the wall of a craft room, consider hanging one or more vertical rods on which to mount wrapping paper, rolls of fabric, or ribbon. Attach a pair of scissors to a string and hang it on a hook next to the rolls so you'll be equipped when you need to cut off some material.

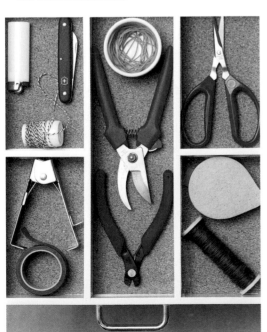

OPPOSITE PAGE Glass-front drawers will save you from rummaging through hidden contents to find what you're looking for. Over a long wooden countertop, hanging rolls of paper make for quick gift wrapping.

LEFT Store stationery and ribbon in labeled, lidded boxes.

BELOW LEFT Craft tools are kept organized and protected with drawer dividers and soft cork lining.

BELOW RIGHT Abundant natural light, plus tables and carts on wheels, makes this an ideal craft room for painting.

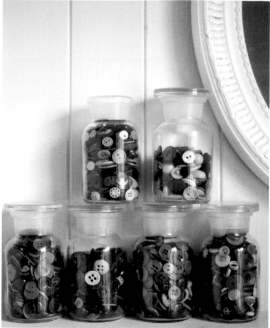

Sewing Spaces

The amount of space required for a sewing area depends on the level of use. If you're an avid quilter or love to make your own clothes and decorative furnishings for the home, then you'll want to organize the area carefully so that it's a comfortable place to work for extended periods and one in which you can easily set hands on your tools and accessories. Check out the chapter on home offices for additional ideas. On the other hand, if you sew only occasionally—to hem a pair of pants, for instance—you may prefer the sewing machine stashed in a closet, with a couple of transportable toolboxes for your accessories. These can be moved to the home office or the kitchen table for that occasional project.

Professional organizer Monica Ricci had a client who was a crafter and needed help organizing her fabric and notions. Ricci used fishing tackle boxes to store all the small items. "They're great for crafts because they are portable and have all those little trays," Ricci says. She suggests sorting fabric scraps by size and color, then storing them in clear plastic tubs. "If they are organized by size, you'll know if you have what you need for the next project." Large stacking bins can also be useful if you have lots of fabric scraps. Just label each bin with the sizes and colors they contain. Bolts of fabric can be hung vertically on the wall inside a closet.

TOP LEFT Clear glass jars keep mending materials assembled, portable, and visible.

TOP RIGHT Reuse vintage glass bottles to keep spare buttons sorted by style or color.

BOTTOM LEFT Wall hooks and a metal dress form allow you to step back and examine your creations.

The combination of natural and direct light over this office desk makes it suitable as a craft or sewing area as well.

Chapter 10

Getting It Done

Now that you have considered some ideas for the rooms you plan to reorganize, you're ready to get started in earnest. If you're still not sure where to begin, you may want to enlist the help of a professional home organizer or designer. On the following pages, you'll find tips on how to choose and work with professionals. You'll also find ways to keep costs down, learn the latest thinking about storing toxic items, and discover some creative approaches to preserving family heirlooms.

The sorting and clearing-out phase may be messy, but the result is an organized space.

Purging and Organizing

Move everything out of the closet or cabinet you're reorganizing to a separate sorting location.

In dealing with any space that has organization problems, your first step should always be to sort through your belongings and get rid of what you no longer need. To skip this step is to risk spending money on storage products that may not solve the problem. If you haven't moved in a while, chances are you're long overdue for a reevaluation of your possessions. It's easy to forget about things in cabinets and closets that you rarely open. You may also be cramming regularly used items into overloaded shelves and drawers. Purging will allow all of the storage spaces in the house to breathe so that everyday items are within sight and accessible.

Staging Areas

Pull out all items in your cabinet or closet and organize them by type. You may choose to do this in the middle of the living room, on the dining room table, or on a bed. Keep like items together and have a separate pile for things you're considering moving to a different part of the house. If you're cleaning out an area that is too full, aim to remove at least a third of the contents. That way, you will have space to eventually grow back to three quarters of what you started with.

Editing the Piles

Be realistic about what you want to keep. The various chapters in this book have discussed the basic needs in individual rooms, but a good general rule is to try to get rid of anything you haven't used or worn in the past year, unless it's something of sentimental value or an item you keep for special occasions. Items you rarely use can be relegated to long-term storage in the garage, basement, or attic. Only things that you need ready at hand should be in the closets, cabinets, and shelves of your home.

Take books and magazines off shelves, then arrange them in piles to help you decide what to keep.

PROFESSIONAL ORGANIZER
SARA EIZEN ON

Making the Time

People get overwhelmed when they think about how many areas need to be reorganized, and they end up never tackling the problem. Instead of figuring out how to complete the project in a day or a weekend, schedule two hours at a time during the next month of Saturdays. Remind yourself that you're working on it for only two hours and then you can go have fun. Chipping away at the problem in small chunks like this will be far less overwhelming.

Getting Rid of It

After you've winnowed out what you no longer need, your goal should be to throw away as little as possible. Once you have a stack of things you're willing to part with, separate that group into piles to be sold, to be given to relatives or friends, to be donated to charity or a local school, or to be recycled. Used electronic equipment, plus old CDs and their cases, can be recycled in many areas. Soiled clothing can be turned into rags for cleaning. Search online for the various recycling options in your community. Once you've decided how to dispose of things, act quickly. Put what you're donating into your car so you have an incentive to drop it off within the next few days. Avoid leaving the dispensible items in your house or you may have a change of heart and tuck them back into a closet.

When you come across an item from your childhood that you didn't know you still had, take a moment to consider whether the item retains any meaning for you. Perhaps after the moment of rediscovery, you will actually be ready to let it go. "I suggest taking a picture of the heirloom so you will always be able to remember it, if keeping the original doesn't make sense," says professional organizer Sara Eizen. Having the photo will make it easier to donate or sell those potentially sentimental items. Let someone else get some use out of them.

Hazardous Items

There are a variety of things that are simply too toxic to donate or throw away. Check with your waste-management company—most have Web sites that list in detail what cannot be put in the trash or the recycling, such as compact fluorescent light bulbs, batteries, adhesives, solvents, standard household cleaners, medications, and some personal-care products. Sign up for the next toxic-waste drop-off near your community and box up the items that fall into these categories so you can dispose of them as soon as possible.

TOP LEFT Make one pile for charity, another pile for friends, and yet another pile for restocking your supply of house-cleaning rags.

TOP RIGHT Maybe it's time to let go of the dress you wore to the homecoming dance in high school.

BOTTOM Question the items you've stashed on high shelves: Will you ever use them again?

Box up the items you'll move to the garage or attic.

Getting Help

Professional organizers and designers will leave you with a well-organized home and systems to help you keep it that way.

For some people, going through the purging process described in the previous pages is not an easy experience. Perhaps things have gotten so radically disorganized that the thought of correcting matters is completely overwhelming. Meanwhile, people who live in very small homes may feel—with some justification—that they literally don't have enough space and are out of options. Still others have strong emotional bonds to their belongings and find the thought of parting with their things particularly difficult.

You can hire a professional to help. Or you can turn to a friend—one who will make you stick to your "purging appointment" and push you on the difficult decisions of what to let go.

PROFESSIONAL ORGANIZERS can help you solve storage and organization problems. Much like personal trainers, they help you reach goals you haven't managed to reach on your own. They do this, in part, by offering an objective perspective on the task at hand. Organizers generally charge by the hour, though some will quote a flat fee for your project. When asked how long a project might take, professional organizer Monica Ricci says it depends on the client. "Dramatic changes can be achieved in a relatively short period of time because of the focus that an organizer creates. Typically an organizer will plan to work with you for at least two hours at a time so that significant progress can be made during each session," Ricci says.

Check out the National Association of Professional Organizers Web site (see Resources, page 186) to search for a professional in your area. Some organizers specialize in particular projects, such as moving, home office organization, or closet design. Some have interior design backgrounds and can help make your space beautiful as well as functional. Interview two or three professionals to find an organizer with whom you feel comfortable. Ask to see photos of their prior work or have them tell you about some particularly unique solutions they've come up with in the past.

The goal of hiring a professional organizer isn't just to solve the immediate problems but to devise systems that allow you to avoid winding up in the same predicament. "That's how I see organizing," explains professional organizer Jen M. R. Doman. "You know what to do, but you're overwhelmed. Whatever the issue is, it probably took years to get that way. In a relatively short amount of time, I can undo what it took years to create and put systems in place to help you maintain it yourself."

Professional organizer Deborah Silberberg sees herself as an advocate for her clients. "Our solutions are highly customized. We try to make the best decision for this particular client in this particular space," Silberberg says.

INTERIOR DESIGNERS are experts on style, color, and texture. If you want to remodel your bathroom or bedroom and need help on paint, flooring, furniture selection, and lighting but you also need some clever organizing solutions to make the room more functional, look for an interior designer who lists organizing as one of the services being offered. Designers can also give your bookshelves a facelift or help create decorative displays with items you already own.

RETAIL SPECIALISTS at storage and home improvement centers can help you figure out closet systems or elements of your storage spaces, such as shelving and hooks. Depending on where you shop, you may find valuable help and advice, but you will be on your own for taking measurements and thinning out your possessions, since these professionals don't generally make house calls.

Budget Solutions

Splurge on a pullout rack in the kitchen and do without the built-ins for other cabinets and drawers.

Perusing the aisles of a store or searching online for storage solutions can give you some great ideas. But as you add items to your basket, you will quickly realize that all of these specialized racks and containers cost a significant sum. While it's true that there are hundreds of store-bought solutions to help with the process, you can achieve some of the same results even if you can't afford them all. Select a small number of these items that will make the biggest impact on your home. A pullout shelf, for example, can make lower cabinets more useful for storage.

Containers and Packing Materials

Professional organizer Sara Eizen suggests watching for sales and buying less expensive containers that aren't necessarily marketed as organizing solutions. "Plastic containers are inexpensive and perfect for storing small things. Use them for anything from toiletries to craft supplies," Eizen says. "And after the holidays you can usually get amazing deals on storage bins."

There are also many ways to get a second use out of packing materials, rather than throwing them away. Bedding often comes in zippered plastic bags that can be used to store seasonal items. Glass jars for pasta sauce can be useful for sewing supplies or cotton swabs in the bathroom. Sturdy ice cream containers can provide a home for ribbon or extra batteries on a shelf in the utility closet. An egg carton is great for jewelry or loose beads. Place an old coffee can on the desk to hold pens or paintbrushes. Bin-type cardboard boxes that you get at bulk grocery stores are sturdy enough for use as toy containers. The possibilities are endless. Before you throw that next container away, take a moment to assess its size, shape, and durability, and think whether or not there is an organizing problem it might help you solve.

PROFESSIONAL ORGANIZER
SYLVIA BORCHERT ON

Label Makers

Any container can be made into an efficient storage solution with the help of a label maker. If you see an opportunity to label large numbers of things, get a label maker with a large keyboard. The small ones tend to be awkward for typing.

TOP Stacked wooden wine crates are turned into bookshelves.

BOTTOM LEFT Fancy food tins can be reused in a bathroom or craft area.

BOTTOM RIGHT Look around the house for boxes, tins, and packing materials that can be used for storage.

ABOVE LEFT Instead of expensive upper cabinets, find wood planks at a salvage yard and L-brackets at a home center to create your own open shelves.

ABOVE RIGHT When a local school was torn down, these lockers were salvaged and put to use as storage in a hallway.

Recycled Materials

Sometimes you need larger containers to solve your storage problems. But instead of buying brand-new shelves, cabinets, or desks, think about the possibilities with used furniture or building materials that can be repurposed to provide a solution.

In salvage yards you will find lumber and molding that can be used to build new bookshelves. A few L-brackets from the hardware store and a piece of old lumber can make a sturdy shelf in a closet. Depending on when you go, your salvage yard may also have old bathroom vanities or kitchen cabinets that can find a second life in a closet, mudroom, or laundry room.

While you're there, look for old window and cabinet hardware. Salvage yards often have large quantities of things like rusted handles and pretty colored glass knobs. Such things can be used in place of hooks on the walls for hanging tea towels in the kitchen or dog leashes in the closet.

Used Office Furniture

Filing cabinets and desks with built-in storage can be costly. If you aren't picky about color or style, look for used office furniture online. In some areas there are also warehouses full of office furniture, usually from companies that have gone out of business. Ergonomic chairs, cabinets, desks,

shelving units, and bulletin boards can be found, often at a steep discount. Think creatively as you wander the aisles; there may be ways you can spruce up what you find. Also consider uses other than what each piece was made for.

Secondhand Stores

Perhaps you wouldn't expect to find storage and organizing solutions at vintage and secondhand furniture stores. But if you look at the shape and size of each item, rather than being limited by its original use, you may discover some interesting options. Wooden soda crates with metal sides are sturdy storage containers—much more unique

than plastic tubs. A turned-wood hanging rack, originally designed for displaying quilts, might easily be repurposed for storing sheets of wrapping paper or bolts of fabric in a craft room. Also look for solid-wood bookshelves that can be brought back to life with a fresh coat of paint, or wooden chests in which to store extra linens at the foot of your bed.

ABOVE LEFT Reuse a ladder or a piece of a metal arbor from the garden to keep newspapers and magazines organized.

ABOVE RIGHT It was once a flat file cabinet in an office. Now it's an end table with storage in a living room.

Specialized Storage

Paint, solvents, and adhesives are best kept in the garage or in a shed, away from living areas.

I tems that you need to store long term, irreplaceable heirlooms, and things that require special protection because of their hazardous nature all require unique storage solutions. Depending on exactly what you're storing, you may have to create a separate space where such specialized needs can be met.

Hazardous Materials

Paints, pesticides, and other toxic products should not be kept in the house. Even with the lids in place, a tiny amount of fumes may emit from the containers, negatively affecting your indoor air quality. Moreover, in the event of an earthquake or fire, certain combinations of chemicals in these products can result in dangerous or highly flammable reactions. If you must keep such items in the home, store them as far away from your living space as possible. Ideally, they should be secured in a locked cabinet so children can't reach them. But read the individual labels to make certain that none of them require storage with ventilation. Anything with this stipulation should absolutely not be stored in the home, because the fumes will make you sick or might spontaneously combust if they are not given proper air transfer. In general, it's a good practice to keep out most flammable substances, as they can make an unrelated fire much more dangerous.

Emergency Supplies

Although it's not a scenario anyone likes to think about, every household should have a store of emergency supplies as a precaution in the event of a natural disaster. Depending on the size of your family, this supply may not be compact. You will need enough food, water, and personal-care products to last three to seven days. If you doubt that you will find the time to assemble your own disaster-readiness kit, look for premade versions online. Be sure it includes the following: first aid kit, flashlight, radio, whistle, batteries, dust masks, can opener, matches, toilet paper, tarp, hand sanitizer, and basic tools. Even with the premade kits, you are sometimes expected to add your own canned food and energy bars, water—at least one gallon per person per day for three days or more—sleeping bags, and a solar cell phone charger. Also consider including prescription medications, extra prescription glasses, all essential keys, gas for your automobile, emergency cash, and copies of personal identification and important papers, such as your home insurance policy.

Once you've assembled your emergency supplies, store them in a watertight container.

Assemble all of these items, then look for one or more watertight containers in which to store them. Ideally this container should be kept near the door of the garage. If you don't have a garage, you may need to make room for these supplies in a utility closet or in the basement. Avoid places that have a higher likelihood of being trapped in a building collapse caused by an earthquake or hurricane.

Heirlooms

Sentimental items that you don't bring out on a regular basis require special care in storage. Because you don't see them very often, they are susceptible to damage by bugs or moisture if precautions are not taken. Such items are best kept in the house rather than in the garage, attic, or basement. Like wine, they often benefit from storage away from light and heat. Old fabric and paper should not be kept in cardboard boxes or packing materials that contain acids. If you want to keep these materials in plastic boxes with snap-on lids, so as to protect them from insects, find boxes that are made of polypropylene—marked with a number 5 in the recycling logo. The alternative, PVC, releases chemicals that can cause damage over time. You may also want to consult a professional conservator to learn the best way to protect your treasures. For some heirloom textiles, for example, it's best to keep them in acid-free archival storage boxes that allow a slight amount of air circulation.

Photographs

Many households now have the equipment to scan and digitally enhance old photographs. And it's a useful step to scan your most cherished printed photos and store the files on an external hard drive. You may prefer to hire a teenager to perform this chore for you, or take them to a company that specializes in digital reproduction. Professional organizer Monica Ricci suggests framing printed digital copies if you want the photos on display. "Or, if you prefer to display the originals, make sure you use acid-free matting and backing paper, and ultraviolet-protection glass to keep the images from fading," Ricci advises.

Design consultant Kate Parker uses archival-quality boxes to store original photos. "Take all of your older photos out of the shoeboxes and put them in boxes that are specifically made to preserve these prints; otherwise the colors will quickly fade," Parker advises.

TOP LEFT Antique linens should be stored in acid-free boxes to preserve their integrity.

TOP RIGHT A treasured first edition is preserved in a Lucite box so that air cannot harm the brittle paper.

BOTTOM Transfer old printed photos to archival-quality boxes to prevent them from fading.

OPPOSITE PAGE Use ultraviolet-rated glass to keep delicate artwork and photographs protected from natural or electric light.

Resources

The following retailers, manufacturers, and organizations have the types of storage and display solutions seen and discussed throughout this book.

Beauty Alert
www.beautyalert.biz
Ways to avoid using expired cosmetics

Bed Bath & Beyond
www.bedbathandbeyond.com

CB2
www.cb2.com

California Closets
www.californiaclosets.com
Closet design and products

Closet Factory
www.closetfactory.com
Closet design and products

Closetmaid
www.closetmaid.com
Closet design and products

Closet Works
www.closetworks.com
Closet design and products

The Container Store
www.containerstore.com

Crate & Barrel
ww.crateandbarrel.com

EcoHaul
www.ecohaul.com
San Francisco area socially and environmentally responsible waste removal and disposal solutions

Green Citizen
www.greencitizen.com
San Francisco area recycling centers

Guidecraft
www.guidecraft.com
Kids' furniture

Hable Construction
www.hableconstruction.com

The Home Depot
www.homedepot.com

IKEA
www.ikea-usa.com

Knape & Vogt Manufacturing
www.knapeandvogt.com
Storage and hardware solutions

Kolo
www.kolo.com
Photo albums and boxes

Lowe's
www.lowes.com

**National Association
of Professional Organizers**
www.napo.net

Organize.com
www.organize.com
Household organizing products

The Picturewall Company
www.thepicturewallcompany.com
Picture-hanging templates

Pottery Barn
www.potterybarn.com

Ready America
www.ready.gov
Emergency preparedness and supply kits

Restoration Hardware
www.restorationhardware.com

Rev-A-Shelf
www.rev-a-shelf.com
Cabinet pullouts and accessories

Rubbermaid
www.rubbermaid.com

Schulte Corporation
www.schultestorage.com
Storage and closet products

Space Savers
www.spacesavers.com
Household organizing products

Specialty Plastics
www.casesforcollectibles.com
Display cases

Stacks and Stacks
www.stacksandstacks.com
Household organizing products

U.S. Composting Council
www.compostingcouncil.org
National organization promoting composting

West Elm
www.westelm.com

Photography Credits

Melanie Acevedo/Getty Images: 176; Anthony-Masterson/Getty Images: 165; artparadigm/Getty Images: 168 bottom; Edmund Barr: 153 bottom right; Justin Bernhaut/Getty Images: 125 bottom left; Richard Birch/acpsyndication.com/JBG Photo: 57 right, 65; Red Cover/Johnny Bouchier: 23 bottom, 149 bottom; Nick Bowers/acpsyndication.com/JBG Photo: 125 top; Henk Brandsen/taverneagency.com: 56; Rob D. Brodman: 152–153, 154; Hallie Burton/acpsyndication.com/JBG Photo: 112; Sharyn Cairns: 143 bottom left, 47 top, 48 top, 69 top right, 75 right; Sharyn Cairns/acpsyndication.com/JBG Photo: 179 bottom right; Red Cover/Alun Callender: 27 left, 141, 169, 71 top, 71 bottom right; Red Cover/Ginette Chapman: 132 bottom left; Della Chen: 5 center right; Jonn Coolidge/Art Rep Team: 79 top right, 92; Red Cover/Christopher Drake: 107 top; Red Cover/Dan Duchars: 10, 51 bottom, 149 top left; John Dummer/taverneagency.com: 29 top right, 127 right; Hotze Eisma/taverneagency.com: 155 top right; Red Cover/Jake Fitzjones: 14, 25 bottom right, 33 bottom right, 39 top, 118 left; Red Cover/David George: 69 top left; Douglas Gibb/Getty Images: 29 top left; Red Cover/Douglas Gibb: 33 top, 37 bottom left, 59 bottom right, 140 left; Tria Giovan: 42 top, 45, 54 middle, 143 bottom right; Red Cover/Tria Giovan: 63 bottom, 72 top left (designer: jackya@landhamdesigns.com), 81, 90 top, 95, 124 (architect: Lisa Pope Westernman); Thayer Allyson Gowdy: 63 top right, 79 bottom, 85, 99 top, 116, 134 bottom, 135 right, 157 bottom, 159; Anders Gramer/www.sarahkaye.com: 120 left; John Granen: 52, 69 bottom, 140 right, 148, 151 left,

157 top; Art Gray: 74; Margot Hartford: 30 bottom left, 42 bottom right; Ken Hayden: 5 bottom left; Red Cover/Winfried Heinze: 35 left; Joanna Henderson/www.sarahkaye.com: 17 top, 136 top left, 150, 153 top right, 156, 161 right, 174 bottom; Red Cover/Sarah Hogan: 29 bottom right; Maree Homer/acpsyndication.com/JBG Photo: 46, 48 bottom, 59 bottom left, 122, 167 top, 181 left; Johner/Getty Images: 109; Red Cover/Holly Joliffe: 11; courtesy of Kolo (www.kolo.com): 184 bottom; Nathalie Krag/taverneagency.com: 91, 96, 117 top; Julia Kuskin: 71 bottom left; Red Cover/Sandra Lane: 89 bottom left; Dave Lauridsen: 13 top; Andrew Lehmann/acpsyndication.com/JBG Photo: 50, 137; ©Geoff Lung/f8 Photo Library: 41, 72 bottom, 94 right, 172; Dan Magree/acpsyndication.com/JBG Photo: 139 top; Paul Massey/Getty Images: 163 top; Red Cover/Paul Massey: 93 top, 138; Simon McBride/Getty Images: 155 top left; Red Cover/Simon McBride: 39 bottom right, 164 bottom; Ericka McConnell: front cover (styling: Philippine Scali; Trivino Binder and Havana Archival Box courtesy of Kolo, Kolo.com), 21 (spice rack: www.deandeluca.com), 25 top, 25 bottom left, 27 right (cleaning products and props courtesy of www.mrsmeyers.com and www.caldrea.com), 30 bottom right (spice rack: www.deandeluca.com), 47 bottom, 54 top, 84 top, 90 middle (Hideaway Storage Boxes: www.hableconstruction.com; bedding: www.ericatanov.com), 100 bottom, 103 bottom (Storage Boxes and Bushel: www.hableconstruction.com; basket: www.atomicgardenoakland.com), 115 middle, 125 bottom right (basket: www.atomicgardenoakland.com),

162, 163 bottom, 168 top left, 182, 183 (matchstick bottle designed by Jen Pearson, available at www.atomicgardenoakland.com), 187; William Meppem/acpsyndication.com/JBG Photo: 111; Red Cover/Karyn Millet: 19, 39 bottom left; Minh + Wass: 98–99, 101, 107 bottom; Ngoc Minh Ngo: 31, 40 bottom left; Red Cover/James Mitchell: 83 left; Laura Moss: 9 bottom left, 42 bottom left, 67, 79 top left, 97 top, 103 top, 104 top left, 104 top right, 126, 179 bottom left; courtesy of potterybarn.com: 33 bottom left, 48–49, 64 bottom, 134 top, 136 bottom, 144 top, 144 bottom, 151 right; Richard Powers/www.sarahkaye.com: 15, 75 left, 83 right, 131 bottom, 136 top right, 139 bottom left, 142, 173, 179 top right, 184 top right; Red Cover/Practical Pictures: 78; Red Cover/David Prince: 13 bottom, 62; Amanda Prior/acpsyndication.com/JBG Photo: 175; Red Cover: 102; Red Cover/Ed Reeve: 132 bottom right; Robert Reichenfeld/acpsyndication.com/JBG Photo: 7; Laura Resen/Art Rep Team: 23 top, 37 right, 53 bottom, 61, 68 top, 68 bottom, 76 bottom, 89 top, 106, 118 right, 119 top, 129, 139 bottom right, 147; Red Cover/James Robinson: 117 bottom; Alexandra Rowley: 8, 120 right, 131 top, 178; Red Cover/Paul Ryan-Goff: 24, 123 bottom; Christian Sarramon: 171; Annie Schlechter/Art Rep Team: 16, 17 bottom left, 94 bottom left, 110, 115 top; Rob Shaw/acpsyndication.com/JBG Photo: 100 top; Jen Siska: 40 bottom right, 66, 73, 90 bottom; Red Cover/Evan Sklar: 9 bottom right; Rhiannon Slatter/acpsyndication.com/JBG Photo: 105; Thomas J. Story: 9 top, 12–13, 30 top left, 35 right (Buttrick Wong Architects), 36, 38 (Kelly Barthelemy Design), 40 top,

53 top, 58 (designer: James Trewitt; architect: E. J. Meade), 63 top, 64 top, 70, 72 top right, 76 top right, 80 left, 82, 84 bottom, 89 bottom right, 94 top left, 104 bottom, 123 top, 130, 132 top, 133, 135 left, 143 top, 144–45 (www.parisrenfroedesign.com), 155 bottom, 160, 161 left, 167 bottom left, 180 right, 185; Tim Street-Porter: 26 right, 119 bottom, 166; Red Cover/Trine Thorsen: 18; ©Debi Treloar/Livingetc/IPC+ Syndication: 76 top left; Red Cover/Chris Tubbs: 29 bottom left, 80 right (designer: Maiden), 97 bottom right, 189; Jo Tyler/www.sarahkaye.com: 99 bottom, 149 top right, 167 bottom right, 168 top right, 180 left, 181 right; Alexander van Berge/taverneagency.com: 127 left; Mikkel Vang/taverneagency.com: 37 top left, 57 left, 87, 88; Dominique Vorillon: 51 top; Julian Wass: 22, 97 bottom left; Michael Wee/acpsyndication.com/JBG Photo: 77; Red Cover/Deborah Whitlaw-Llewellyn LLC: 28; Michele Lee Willson: 34 left (design: Brian Eby), 34 right, 43 (cabinets & wall panels: Michael Meyer Fine Woodworking; building contractor: Bay West Builders; architect: William Duff Architects), 54 bottom (design: Kathryn Rogers), 55, 113, 114, 115 bottom; Alex Wilson/Getty Images: 59 top; Andrew Wood/Getty Images: 32; Red Cover/Andrew Wood: 26 left; Polly Wreford/www.sarahkaye.com: 1, 93 bottom, 121, 164 top left, 164 top right, 174 top left, 174 top right, 184 top left; Hans Zeegers/taverneagency.com: 17 bottom right

Index

A

Accessories, for organizing, 25, 121
Accessories and jewelry, 80, 94, 123
Appliance garages, 43, 140
Appliances, specialty, 43
Armoires, 17, 100, 117, 119, 144
Art and objects
  collections, 70–73, 90
  heirlooms and keepsakes, 184
  photographs, 82–85, 107, 131, 184
  See also Display, options for
Audio and video equipment, 64–65

B

Baskets and bins
  for food items, 34
  on open shelving, 40
  for pet food and supplies, 23
  for toiletries and towels, 11, 47, 48, 51, 54
  for toys and games, 14, 67, 102, 103
  for under-bed storage, 90
  for under-sink storage, 27
  for under-table storage, 63
  See also Containers
Bathrooms
  freestanding furniture in, 10, 50–51
  laundry and trash containers, 56–57
  towels, 11, 50–54, 57
  tub and shower areas, 58–59
  vanities, 46–49
Bedrooms
  built-in cabinets for, 15
  closets, 17, 116–123
  displaying art and objects, 89, 90, 94
  furniture, 93, 117
  health considerations for, 89
  as personal retreats, 88–95
  reading areas in, 94, 95
  work spaces in, 93, 138–139
Beds, 97, 104
Benches, 51, 150
Bicycles, 13

Books and magazines, 74–77, 173
Bookshelves
  in bathrooms, 51
  budget solutions for, 180, 181
  in gathering areas, 74–77, 79
  in guest rooms, 97
  in home offices, 137
  in kitchens, 40
  as work spaces, 97
Borchert, Sylvia (professional organizer), 5, 33, 43, 53, 107, 113, 132, 151, 163
Boxes, 72, 77, 91, 100
  See also Containers
Budget considerations, 117, 178–181
Built-ins, 15, 17, 66, 118, 152
Bulletin and message boards, 23, 137

C

Cabinets
  in bathrooms, 46–49, 54
  in bedrooms, 15
  china, 79, 80
  in entryways, 152, 154
  in kitchens, 25, 34, 38, 39, 43
  in walk-in closets, 118, 119
Caddies, bath and shower, 48, 59
CDs and DVDs, 64
Children
  bathrooms for, 53
  bedrooms for, 102–107
  closets for, 17, 124–125
  coat hooks and racks for, 151, 152
  craft areas for, 80
  kitchen safety, 27, 28, 39
  toy and game storage, 14, 66–67, 102, 103, 104
Cleaning supplies, 26, 27, 115, 163
Closets
  alternatives to, 17, 100, 104
  bedroom, 116–123
  entryway, 16
  hall and utility, 114–115
  as home offices, 132, 139, 144
  reorganizing, 110–111, 113
  for teens, 126–127
  walk-in, 118–119, 121–123, 125, 127
Closet systems, 112–113, 118, 157, 165, 177

Clothing
  care of, 164
  disposal of unwanted, 111
  folded storage, 120
  hangers for, 117, 120, 121
  hanging storage, 120, 121
  organizing process for, 110–111, 117, 126–127
  seasonal and special-occasion, 120, 121
  sports and dance, 127
Coat racks, 151, 155
Collections, 68, 70–73, 90
Color, organizing by, 53, 71
Containers
  for archival storage, 184
  boxes, 72, 77, 91, 100
  budget solutions for, 179, 181
  for craft supplies, 168
  for emergency supplies, 183
  for hazardous materials, 183
  for home offices, 135, 139
  jewelry boxes, 94
  for small items, 124, 125
  See also Baskets and bins
Cookware, 26, 27, 28, 30–31
Countertops
  bathroom, 48
  kitchen, 24, 25, 37, 43
  in laundry and craft rooms, 161
Craft spaces, 80, 114, 166–169
Cubbies, 77, 104, 120, 152

D

Davey, Kit (interior designer), 4, 10, 39, 48, 63, 67, 70, 75, 76, 117, 120, 131, 135, 155
Dennis, Lori (interior designer), 5, 35, 40, 72, 80, 89, 100, 104, 115, 138, 139, 151, 163
Dining rooms, 12, 79–81, 139
Dishware and glasses, 28, 40, 79, 80
Display, options for
  in bathrooms, 51, 59
  in bedrooms, 89, 90, 94
  in children's rooms, 100, 106–107
  collections, 68, 70–73
  dishware and glasses, 9, 40, 42
  in kitchens, 40
  photographs, 83, 84, 85
  See also Art and objects

Doman, Jen M. R. (professional organizer), 5, 9, 25, 37, 54, 57, 64, 67, 90, 93, 123, 125, 177
Donating unwanted items, 23, 75, 111, 174
Doors
  cabinet, glass, 8, 38, 40, 42, 43
  closet, 122, 123, 125
  hanging racks for, 103, 115, 123, 125
Drawers
  for craft materials, 80, 167
  dividers for, 25, 28, 47, 94, 99, 137
  junk, 25
  in kitchens, 30, 31, 38, 39, 42, 43
  in walk-in closets, 118
Dressing areas, 51

E

Eizen, Sara (professional organizer), 5, 18, 26, 27, 47, 84, 106, 115, 117, 135, 173, 174, 179
Electronic equipment, 64–65, 131
Emergency supplies, 183
Entryways, back door, 154–155
Entryways, front door, 148–153
Environmental considerations, 26, 40, 164
Ergonomics, 132
Exercise equipment, 97

F

Family rooms. *See* Gathering areas
Filing systems, 134–135
Fireplaces and mantels, 68
Food storage, 25, 34, 35, 37
Frames, picture, 83, 84
Furniture
  for children's rooms, 98–99, 104
  freestanding, 50–51, 100, 104, 117, 118, 124
  multipurpose, 93, 151
  used, 180–181

G

Gardening equipment, 156, 157
Gathering areas
  audio and video equipment, 64–65

bookshelves, 74–77
dining rooms, 79–81
display, 70–73, 82–85
family rooms, 13
fireplaces and mantles, 68
games and toys, 66–67
living rooms, 13, 138, 139
strategies for small spaces, 63
Glassware. *See* Dishware and
glasses
Grouping, 39, 47, 113, 115
Guest rooms, 96–97, 138–139

H

Hall closets, 114–115
Hallways, 143
Hangers, 117, 120, 121, 164
Hanging-rail systems, 26
Hazardous items, 174, 183
Health considerations
for bedrooms, 89
ergonomics, 132
kitchen sink area, 26, 47
medicines and personal-care
products, 47, 54
for nurseries, 98
Heirlooms and keepsakes, 184
Home offices. *See* Offices, home
Hooks
in bathrooms, 11, 51
in entryways, 16, 151
in hall and utility closets, 115
in laundry rooms, 163

I–K

Interior designers, 177
Islands, kitchen, 36–37
Jewelry, 94
Keys, 25, 149
Kitchens
cabinets, 8, 25
cookware storage, 26, 28,
30–31
countertops, 24, 25, 139
designing new spaces, 38–43
dish and glassware storage,
28
drawers, 25
food storage, 30–31
islands, 8, 36–37
open shelving, 9, 40
organizing solutions for,
22–23
pantries, 9, 34–35
sink clutter, 26
trash containers, 34–35

under-sink storage, 27
wine storage, 32, 33

L

Labeling, 47, 90, 99, 103, 115,
125
Laundry areas, 157, 160–165
Laundry baskets, 57, 93, 127
Lazy Susans, 25, 33
Lighting, 167, 169
Living rooms. *See* Gathering
areas

M, N

Mail, 25, 149, 152
Maintenance considerations,
40, 72, 151
Medicines, 47
Message and bulletin boards,
23, 137
Mudrooms, 156–157
Multimedia equipment, 64–65
Musical instruments, 67
National Association of Profes-
sional Organizers, 177
No-shoe policy, 151
Nurseries, 98–101

O

Offices, home
filing systems, 134–135
organizing solutions, 136–137,
144
purging and sorting, 130–133
Organizers, professional, 113,
177
Ottomans, 63

P

Pantries, 9, 34–35
Paperwork, 131, 134–135, 140
Parker, Kate (design consultant),
5, 14, 71, 75, 89, 104, 111,
117, 139, 143, 149, 167, 184
Pegboard, 115
Personal-care products, 47, 48,
51, 54–55, 59
Pets, 23, 39
Photographs, 82–85, 107, 131,
184
Pot racks, 26
Professionals, working with,
176–177
Purging, 23, 75, 111, 127,
172–175

R

Racks
for drying laundry, 164
hanging, 26
magazine, 98
shoe, 103, 123
towel, 53, 58
Reading areas, 80, 94, 95
Recycling
kitchen storage for, 34–35
of unwanted items, 111,
120, 174
using salvaged materials,
120, 180
Refrigerators, 33, 37
Retail specialists, 177
Ricci, Monica (professional
organizer), 4, 25, 43, 63,
70, 80, 90, 115, 127, 164,
168, 177, 184
Rods, closet, 118, 127

S

Safety considerations
for children, 27, 28, 98–99
emergency supplies, 183
hazardous materials, 183
personal-care products, 47
Salvaged materials, 120, 180
Schedules, for organizing
projects, 111, 173
Seasonal items, 23, 152
Seating, 39, 80, 95
Selling unwanted items, 111,
174
Sewing spaces, 168–169
Shelving
for bathrooms, 51, 53, 59
for children's rooms, 14,
103, 104
closet systems, 113
for dining rooms, 79
for display, 13, 71, 85, 90, 100
for hall and utility closets,
115
for home offices, 137
for kitchens, 28, 37, 38
for laundry rooms, 161, 163
for mudrooms, 157
pullout, 25, 33, 34, 47, 54
recessed, 55, 59, 163
for work spaces, 19
See also Bookshelves
Shoe racks, 103, 123
Shoes and boots, 123, 151,
152, 155

Silberberg, Deborah (profes-
sional organizer), 5, 28, 39,
135, 164, 177
Silverware and knives, 28
Sink areas, 11, 26, 37, 47, 161
Sleep spaces, 88–95, 96
Small spaces, 13, 63, 66, 89,
104, 142–145
Sorting, 57, 111, 117, 130–133,
172–175
Spices, 26, 30, 31
Systems, closet, 57, 112–113,
118, 165, 177
Systems, organizing, 39, 157,
165, 167

T

Teens, 126–127
Tejada, Celia (Pottery Barn
Creative Director), 4, 51,
64, 83, 136
Templates, photo arrangement,
84, 85
Themes, for collections, 71
Toiletries, 47, 48, 51, 54–55, 59
Towel racks, 53, 58
Towels, 51, 52–54, 57
Toxic waste, disposal of, 174
Toys and games, 14, 66–67, 102,
103, 104
Trash cans, 34–35, 57
Tub and shower areas, 58–59

U–Z

Umbrellas, 152
Under-bed storage, 90, 97
Under-sink storage, 11, 47
Utensils, kitchen, 26, 28
Utility closets, 114–115
Vanities, 46–49
Ventilation, 161
Washers and dryers, 161
Wine, 9, 32–33
Work spaces
in bedrooms, 93, 138–139
decorative solutions for,
18–19, 130–131
in dining rooms, 80, 140
hidden, 144
hiding, concealing, 144
home offices, 130–137
kitchen, 24–27, 37, 39, 140
in living rooms, 138–139
under stairs, 140
study areas in kids' rooms,
104

Sunset guides you to a fabulous home—inside and out

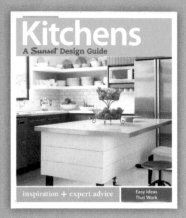

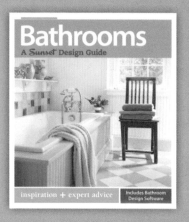

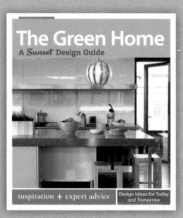

Sunset's all-new Design Guides have everything you need to plan—and create—the home of your dreams. Each book includes advice from top professionals and hundreds of illustrative photos. With an emphasis on green building materials and techniques, this entire series will inspire ideas both inside and outside of your home.

Sunset

Available wherever books are sold.
Visit us online at Sunsetbooks.com